Beautiful Christmas

Carol Field Dahlstrom

250 Best Ideas for a Memorable Holiday

Carol Field Dahlstrom
Brave Ink Press
Ankeny, Iowa

AUTHOR AND EDITOR
Carol Field Dahlstrom

BOOK DESIGN
Lyne Neymeyer

PHOTOGRAPHY
Pete Krumhardt

Copy Editing: Janet Figg, Jill Philby, Jan Temeyer
Proofreading: Elizabeth Dahlstrom
Recipe Development and Testing: Elizabeth Dahlstrom, Ardith Field, Barbara Hoover, Jennifer Petersen
Props and Location: Roger Dahlstrom
Photography Styling Assistant: Donna Chesnut
Exclusive Artwork: Susan Cornelison
Technical Artwork: Shawn Drafahl
Technical Assistant: Judy Bailey

Thanks to the many people who helped in the making of this book: Elizabeth Dahlstrom,
Michael Dahlstrom, Ardith Field, Kristin Krumhardt, Allison May, Betsy May, Jennifer Petersen, Janet Petersma,
Ann E. Smith, Jan Temeyer

ISBN 0-9679764-3-X
Library of Congress Control Number 2004092746

Printed in the United States of America
First Edition

While all of the projects in this book have been checked and tested, human error can occur. Carol Field Dahlstrom, Inc. and
Brave Ink Press cannot be held responsible for any loss or injury associated with the making of any item in this book.
Carol Field Dahlstrom, Inc. and Brave Ink Press strive to provide high quality products and information that will make your life
happier and more beautiful. Please write or e-mail us with your comments, questions, and suggestions or to inquire about
purchasing books at braveink@aol.com or Brave Ink Press, P.O. Box 663, Ankeny, Iowa 50021. Visit us at www.braveink.com

Author and editor Carol Field Dahlstrom has written, edited, and produced numerous crafts,
decorating, and holiday books as well as children's specialty products for 18 years. She has shared
her love of creating, entertaining, and decorating with audiences throughout the country through
speaking engagements and television appearances. Her products inspire families to spend time
together—creating, learning, and celebrating. She lives in the country with her family where she
writes and designs from her studio.

Look for other books by Carol Field Dahlstrom from Brave Ink Press:
Simply Christmas
Christmas—Make it Sparkle
An Ornament a Day

CHRISTMASTIME IS THE MOST BEAUTIFUL TIME OF YEAR. Evergreens are adorned in glorious lights and shiny ornaments. Gifts are wrapped in brightly colored papers and silky ribbons. Christmas cookies are exquisitely decorated and arranged on pretty plates. Store windows welcome shoppers with enticing holiday fare.

But the lasting beauty of Christmas is something more. You see it in the eyes of friends as they look at your lovely tree. You hear it in the giggles of children as they guess what is inside their packages and in the voice of a neighbor as you bring him unexpected goodies. You even notice it in the smile of a stranger as you pass her on a busy street.

So as you decorate your lovely home, wrap your handmade presents, and bake those special cookies—even when you shop for that last-minute gift—know that you are making the real beauty of Christmas come alive in the hearts of those around you. May you have a Beautiful Christmas.

Carol Field Dahlstrom

Contents

23

50

80

99

109

141

About this Book

In this book you'll find ideas and projects for making crafts, decorating your home, and cooking and baking wonderful holiday treats. To make the best use of your valuable holiday time, we have made the book easy for you to follow.

MAKING THE PROJECTS

Every time you make a project or recipe, look for a complete list of "what you need" and a list of directions under the "what you do" heading. In the general materials list, we oftentimes suggest a specific brand of product and where you can find that item. Most items are easy to find in crafts, discount, fabric, or grocery stores. If an item is unusual, we will sometimes refer you to the sources on page 159 that will give you an address or e-mail so you can order the item you wish. In the directions we sometimes give you step-by-step photos to help show exactly how the project was made.

THE PATTERNS

Most of the patterns in the book are full-size. If the patterns are too large to fit on the page, we have put them on a grid and given a percentage to increase them. Take the pattern to the copy shop and enlarge it to the size indicated. For example, if the pattern is enlarged 200%, it will be twice as big as the one shown on the grid.

SAFETY FIRST

When you are making the projects, always remember safety first. When painting or gluing, use adequate ventilation and follow the manufacturer's instructions on the item. Always use extreme care when using crafts knives or cutters of any type.

stocking pattern

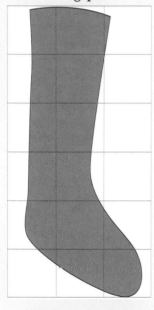

1 square = 1 inch
enlarge 200%

MORE WAYS TO USE THE IDEAS

Many of the projects in the book can be given as Christmas gifts. Look for a *G* for some ideas on making the project into a gift. Some of the projects are so easy they can be made in an evening. Look for an *E* to find these ideas. Some projects are especially fun for families to make together. Look for an *F* to find these items.

THE RECIPES

All of the recipes in this book are family favorites from homes across the country. They have been tested in kitchens just like yours and enjoyed at holiday time. The recipes call for ingredients that are easy to find and available in most parts of the country. The methods are simple to follow and easy to do—even for first time cooks.

BONUS IDEAS

At the end of the chapters, you'll find a list of even more ideas to make your holiday beautiful. These bonus ideas may even spark some more creative projects for you to try.

SCRAPBOOK PAGES

The scrapbook pages on pages 147-152 have call-outs that show what we used on our pages. These lines leading to the item on the page help you identify what makes that page unique.

EXCLUSIVE ART

At the end of the book, you'll find exclusive artwork designed just for you to use in your projects. The artwork is full-size and can be increased or decreased on a color copier to fit your needs. Permission is granted to copy this art for your personal use.

We know you will enjoy making the projects and recipes in this book as you celebrate this most Beautiful Christmas.

Beautifully

stamped

tinseled

glittered

painted

sewn

folded

embellished

jeweled

Elegant Evergreens and Sparkling Ornaments

The center of your holiday decorating is your beautiful Christmas tree. This year create lovely ornaments to adorn your tree that are sure to be treasured for years to come. From feathered beauties and glass painted trims to paper purses and delicate fairy ornaments, you'll find just the inspiration to make your Christmas evergreen more beautiful than ever before.

So Easy

Because there is just one simple step to making these trims, you'll have a tree that Mother Nature would be proud of in no time.

What you need:
- **Purchased matte finish gold ornaments**
- **Tumbler**
- **Tiny feathers (available at crafts stores)**
- **Tacky crafts glue**

FEATHERED FANCIES

Let nature lend a hand in creating these lovely ornaments. Layer soft, textured feathers on the top of simple gold balls to create a stunning effect.

What you do:

Be sure the ornament is clean and dry. Place the gold ornament in the tumbler to support it while you work. Arrange one layer of feathers around the top of the ornament and glue in place. Allow to dry. Arrange another layer of feathers on top of the first layer and glue in place. Allow to dry.

ACORN AND BERRY TRIMS

The mighty oak tree provides the inspiration and the shapely acorns for this clever set of trims.

✳ What you do for the Acorn Ornaments:

Be sure the acorns are clean and free of dirt. Remove the cap of the acorn and drill two holes in the top of the cap about ¼-inch apart. Remove the wire hanger from the gold ball ornament. Put the hanger into the acorn top through the drilled holes and secure underneath. Glue the acorn top to the top of the gold ball. Allow to dry. Hang on the tree with gold ribbon.

✳ What you do for the Acorn and Berry Garland:

Be sure the acorns are clean and free of dirt. If any of the acorn tops are loose, glue them to the acorn bottoms and allow to dry. Drill the acorns and the berries through the center using the drill. Thread the floss onto the needle and string the acorns and fruit. Tie at each end.

✳ What you need for the Ornaments:
- **Small purchased gold ornament**
- **Large acorns**
- **¹⁄₁₆-inch drill bit and drill**
- **Strong crafts glue such as E6000**
- **Gold ribbon**

✳ What you need for the Garland:
- **Large acorns**
- **Tacky crafts glue**
- **Artificial berries**
- **¹⁄₁₆-inch drill bit and drill**
- **Dental floss**
- **Large needle**

There is nothing more lovely than deep red roses and sparkling crystal diamonds.

Add some purple grapes and a touch of sugar and you have a garland that will make your tree a real gem.

12

GRAPES AND ROSES GARLAND

**What you do:**

Cut off the tops of the roses and place in water. Set aside. Remove the individual grapes from the bunch and set aside. Thread the needle with the floss. Leave about an 8-inch piece of floss for hanging and tie a bead on at this point. String the roses by running the needle through the green part of the rose base. Continue stringing the roses, grapes, and crystal beads in desired order. When the desired length is done, finish with a bead and secure. Paint edges of roses with egg white and dip in sugar if desired. The roses will stay fresh on the tree for only a day or two, but will dry nicely during the season and can be used as a dried garland year after year.

❄️**What you need:**
- **Fresh red roses**
- **Scissors**
- **Bowl of water**
- **Artificial sugared soft-plastic grapes (available at crafts stores)**
- **Needle**
- **Dental floss**
- **Crystal beads**
- **Sugar; egg white (optional)**

AQUA ROSE

Remove the top of a clear glass ornament and fill half full with water. Gently push a sweetheart rose bud and a few tiny leaves into the ornament opening. Replace the cap and add a gold ribbon. Display on a clear glass candle holder.

All dressed up with pretty purses and sparkling crystals, this evergreen is ready for the holidays.

14

FANCY PAPER POCKETBOOK

What could be prettier than a tree filled with fancy purses? Choose your favorite style of purse, some elegant papers and trims and you'll have a tree full of treasures.

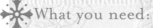

✳ What you do:

Trace around desired patterns from *pages 18-19* on tracing paper and cut out. Fold printed paper in half and place the bottom dotted line of pattern on the fold. Trace onto printed paper and cut out, cutting only one flap where indicated. Score and fold on all lines indicated. For handles, punch holes and add eyelets if desired or glue cording under the top flap. Add a small amount of tissue between layers and glue the purse edges together. Use a clothespin to hold the edges while the glue is drying if necessary. Thread the cording or ribbon through the punched holes and tie as a holder. Add embellishments around the edges and at the clasp if desired.

continued on page 16

✳ What you need:
- **Tracing paper**
- **Pencil**
- **Printed art or scrapbook papers**
- **Scissors**
- **Paper punch**
- **Eyelets and eyelet tools (optional)**
- **Tissue paper**
- **Crafts glue**
- **Clothespin (optional)**
- **Cording or ribbon**
- **Embellishments such as jewels, fabric trims, and buttons**

Use buttons, vintage pins, rhinestones, cording, and other sparkly trims to make each purse have its own personality.

TEARDROP TRIM AND PASTEL GARLAND

Enjoying the sparkle of the holidays, this glass teardrop is topped off with a simple vintage earring and surrounds itself with pastel roses.

❋ What you do:

For the teardrop trim, thread the fine wire through the small hole at the top of the crystal and around the earring. Tie the ribbon around the earring clip. Clip to the tree using the earring clip.

For the pastel garland shown on the tree on pages 14–15 and above, refer to the directions for the Grapes and Roses Garland on *page 12*. String only the pastel rose heads on the floss and hang on the tree.

❋ What you need for the Teardrop Trim:
- **Purchased glass chandelier crystal (available at home centers)**
- **Single clip earring**
- **Fine wire**
- **Sheer ribbon**

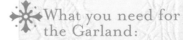

❋ What you need for the Garland:
- **Pastel roses**
- **Floss; needle**

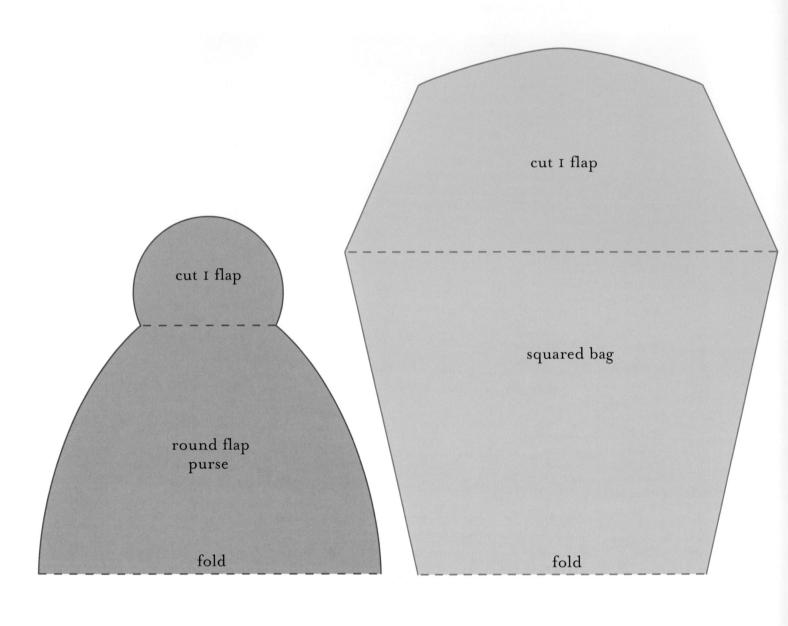

cut I flap

cut I flap

squared bag

round flap
purse

fold

fold

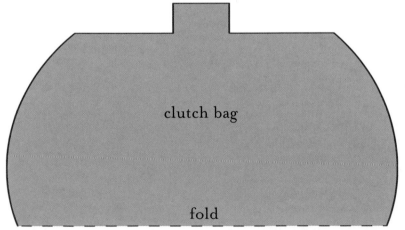

clutch bag

fold

18

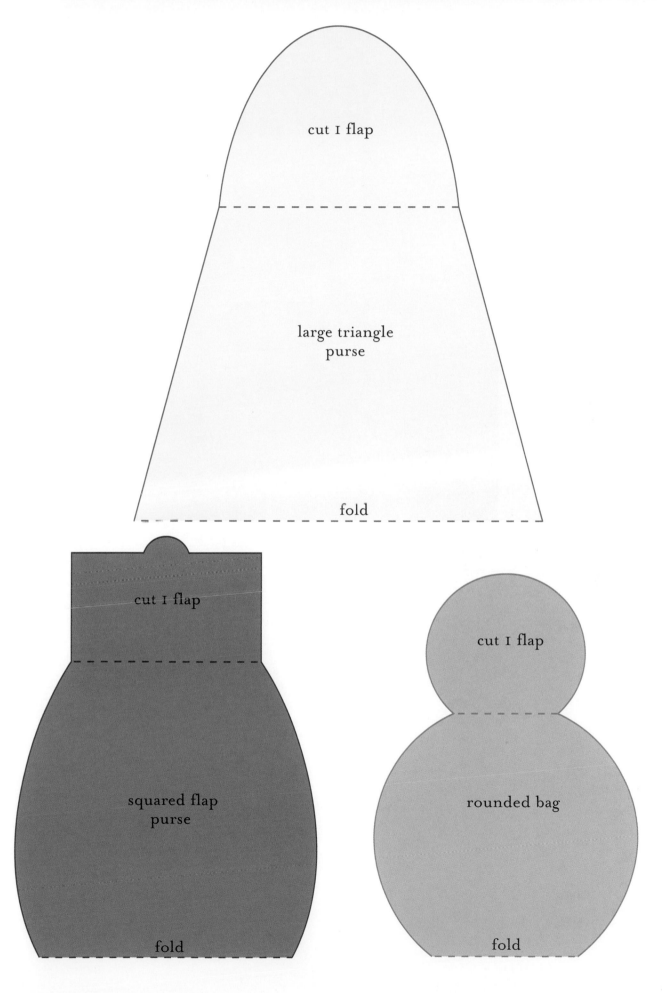

cut I flap

large triangle
purse

fold

cut I flap

squared flap
purse

fold

cut I flap

rounded bag

fold

19

All That Glitters

Embellish your favorite color of ornament with a simple design drawn with glue and dusted with fine glitter. We used clear crafts glue in a bottle with a tiny spout to draw geometric shapes on our Pretty Lavender Ornaments and then dusted them with silver glitter. The Seafoam Green Trim uses green glitter and purchased stickers. We used a wide paintbrush to paint the glue on the All-in-Stripes ornaments and added a dusting of iridescent glitter.

A touch of glitter, a bit of glue, and the magic of pretty stickers is all it takes to make these ornaments sparkle with the season.

21

What you need:

- **Washcloth or small towel**
- **Large clear glass ornament**
- **Copper-color dimensional paint in a tube**
- **Glass paints in red and green**
- **Paintbrushes**
- **Fine iridescent glitter**

PRETTY POINSETTIA BALL

Almost as pretty as the real thing, this sparkling poinsettia is created with transparent glass paints.

What you do:

Be sure the ornament is clean and dry. Rest the ornament on the washcloth to keep it from rolling while you work on it. On one side of the ornament, draw a simple outline of a poinsettia flower with three sets of leaves using the dimensional paints. Add the veins of the flower and leaves. Allow to dry. Use a paintbrush to paint in the center of the leaves using green glass paints. Fill in the center of the poinsettia flower with red glass paint. Sprinkle with glitter while still wet. Allow to dry.

To Give

For an unexpected and much appreciated surprise, present this poinsettia ornament in a small gift box tucked into a blooming red poinsettia plant. The lucky receiver of this gift will have two lovely flowers for the holiday season.

STRIPES AND DOTS

Add the unexpected color of orange to a red Christmas ball and make it glisten with dots of pretty glitter.

What you do:

Be sure the ornament is clean and dry. Place the ornament in the tumbler to keep it stable.

Starting at the neck of the ornament, paint a stripe from the top to the bottom. Work on one side at a time and allow to dry. Use the glitter glue to make dots down the painted stripe. Repeat for the other side. Allow to dry.

What you need:
- **Purchased red ornaments**
- **Glass tumbler**
- **Orange glass paint**
- **Small paintbrush**
- **Red glitter glue**

23

DAINTY MONEY POUCH

What a fun surprise to find this sweet ornament filled with money hanging on a frosty evergreen.

❄ What you need:

- **Tracing paper**
- **Pencil**
- **Scrap of velveteen print fabric**
- **Lining to match fabric**
- **Thread to match fabrics**
- **7 inch piece of black cording**

❄ What you do:

Trace the pattern, *below*, onto tracing paper and cut out. Cut two patterns each from fabric and lining. With right sides together, stitch each set of lining and fabric pieces together at the top edge from markings across top to marking on other side using ³⁄₈-inch seams. Trim, clip at points and across whole top, curved edge. Turn right side out and press.

Pin cording handle to top edge of back side of one pouch, having ends extend out seam allowance. With right sides together, stitch the two pouches together at side and lower edges, catching in the handle at top edges. Backstitch at ends of seams to secure handle. Turn right side out and press.

❄ *To Give*

Think of all the things you could tuck into this pretty holiday pouch—wrapped candies, money, tickets to an event, old photos, tiny antiques, jewelry, a single cookie or truffle in a parchment envelope—even a list of things that you love most about that special person.

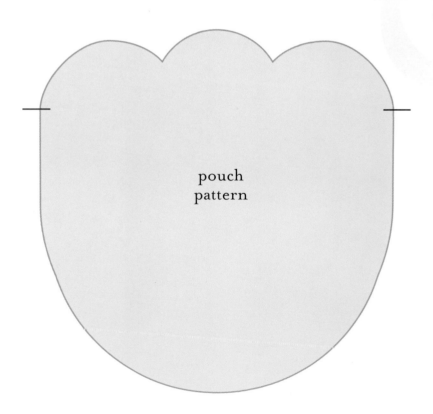

pouch pattern

What you need:
- **Small plastic doll shoes (available at discount and toys stores in packages)**
- **Drill and ¹⁄₁₆-inch drill bit**
- **Waxed dental floss; needle**

DOLLY TRIMS

A girl can never have enough shoes! String those adorable little doll shoes to make a simple garland that the kids will love!

What you do:

Drill a hole through each shoe near the top so shoes will hang evenly. Wipe excess plastic dust off shoes. Thread the needle and string the floss through the holes of the shoes alternating with desired beads. Tie to secure at each end leaving enough floss for tying to the tree. Space the shoes so colors and styles mix with some small and some large shoes alternating with the beads.

GIRLY GARLAND

Colorful hair accessories become a clever garland for the holidays and every little girl will want to keep just a trim or two. Loop together covered rubber bands, criss-cross bright bobby pins, and add some glittered hair clips to make this tree a girl's favorite!

GIFTY ORNAMENTS

Tie two faux gifts together and drape them over an evergreen branch for a pretty Christmas trim.

✳ **What you need:**
- **Two 1-inch wooden blocks**
- **Colored tissue paper**
- **1 yard silver fiber**
- **1 yard iridescent fiber**
- **Transparent tape**

✳ What you do:

Wrap the wooden blocks in tissue paper, as if wrapping a present, taping ends closed with transparent tape. Using both the silver and iridescent fibers at once, start at one end of the yard and tie the fibers around one box, leaving enough fibers to tie a bow. Tie the fiber trims into a bow; secure tightly. (One tail of the bow should be the end of the fibers. The other end will contain the rest of the yard.) With the long fibers that are connected to the first box, start at the opposite end and tie the fibers around the second box as for the first box tying a bow at the end. Secure tightly. The length of fibers remaining between the two wrapped presents will be used to drape the presents over a tree branch.

JINGLE BELL TRIMS

Polka-dotted and jingling all the way, these trims are sure to signal that Christmas is near.

❄ What you do:

Be sure the glass ornament is clean and dry. Pour the paint onto the plate. Dip the eraser end of the pencil into the paint and polka-dot the ornament. Sprinkle with glitter. Allow to dry. Remove the top of the ornament. String the jingle bells onto the chenille stem, coil it, and put inside the glass ball. Replace the top.

❄ What you need:
- **Clear glass ornaments**
- **Air dry glass paint in desired colors**
- **Disposable plate**
- **Pencil with new eraser**
- **Chenille stems**
- **Small jingle bells**
- **Fine gold glitter**

So Easy

❄ *Glass ornaments are inexpensive and readily available at crafts and discount stores. Let the kids help put the bells on the pipe cleaners and you'll make a dozen of these jingle bell trims in an evening.*

What you need for the Anklet Trims:

- **Newborn anklets (vintage or new)**
- **Spray starch**
- **¼-inch ribbon in pastel pink, blue, and yellow**
- **Scissors**
- **Tissue paper**

What you need for Bottle Garland:

- **Purchased tiny baby bottles (available at discount stores in the novelty/wedding section)**
- **Pastel colored sugars**
- **¼-inch ribbon in pastel pink, blue, and yellow**
- **Scissors**

What you need for the Paper Trims:

- **Images of baby cards, vintage or new**
- **Decorative-edged scissors**
- **Cardstock in pastel colors**
- **Glue stick**
- **Paper punch**
- **¼-inch ribbon in pastel pink, blue, and yellow**
- **Scissors**

BABY'S FIRST TREE

All trims in pink and blue make this tree designed to celebrate any new baby. Add gifts of folded money in the stockings to make the little one's piggy bank grow.

What you do for the Anklet Trims:

Wash the stocking and iron using spray starch. Turn the cuff down. Slightly stuff the stocking with tissue paper. Make a tiny bow with the ribbon and sew to the cuff. Sew another piece of ribbon to both sides of the cuff for hanging. Add folded money as a gift in the stocking if desired.

What you do for the Bottle Garland:

Fill the baby bottles with different colors of sugar. Tie the bottles together using the pastel ribbon. Add another ribbon bow around each bottle. Tie on the tree.

What you do for the Paper Trims:

Color copy the images or cut the images to the desired size. Measure around the card and cut the cardstock slightly larger using the decorative-edged scissors. Glue the papers together. Punch holes at the top corners of the paper and thread the ribbon through the holes for hanging.

Simply Stamped

Rubber stamps come in all sizes and in a variety of patterns including letters and numbers. Choose tiny stamps, pretty colors of ink, and fine glitter to make these simple and intricate holiday trims.

The trick to stamping a rounded ornament is to dip the stamp onto the ink pad and then gently rock it back and forth on the surface of the ball. We chose tiny rubber stamps in patterns and letters to make the Silver Leaf Trims, Namesake Ornaments, and the Christmas Motif Trims. Dust the stamped image with glitter while it is still wet. The ink dries quickly, but let it dry completely before working on the other side. Group the ornaments for a showy display.

To Give

✳ *These hand-stamped trims make wonderful gifts. Personalize the ornament using alphabet stamps or choose a stamp ink color that fits the color scheme of the person who is lucky enough to receive this clever trim.*

* What you need for the cookies:
  * Frosted cookies (see page 128-129 for complete instructions)
  * (to order cookie cutters, see Holiday Sources, page 159)
  * ¼-inch satin ribbon

* What you need for Posie Bouquets:
  * Fresh flowers
  * Water tubes to fit flowers (available at florist shops)
  * Satin ribbon
  * Fine wire (optional)

FAIRYLAND TREE

Sweet fairies, butterflies, and dragonflies land on this elegant tree holding beautiful bunches of posies. A tree topper of flowers and ribbon make this tree almost magic!

What you do for the cookies:

To make the cookies, see recipe and instructions on *pages 128-129*. The fairy cookies were made by combining a ballerina cookie cut out and a butterfly cookie cut out. When hanging the cookies on the tree, be sure the holes are made before baking. Thread the ribbon through the holes and tie a knot behind each hole in the cookie.

What you do for the Posie Bouquets:

Cut the flowers to an even length. Fill the floral tubes with water and put the ends of the flowers in the tubes. More than one flower may be able to fit in the tube, depending on the size of the stem. Group the flowers and tie together with a ribbon and bow. Place in the tree, wiring in place, if necessary.

To Give

* *For a special holiday gift, tuck a single ballerina cookie into a parchment envelope and give to your favorite little dancer.*

HOLIDAY HOLLY

A favorite holiday motif, holly comes in all kinds of colors and shapes. Use different kinds of glass paints to make this holly come alive on a purchased ornament.

What you do:

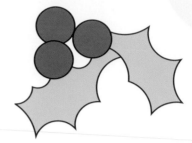

With silver dimensional paint, and referring to pattern, *right,* draw the outline of the holly leaves and berries in small clusters around the frosted ball. Work on one side at a time. Let dry. Using the paint brush, paint in the inside areas of the leaves with green glass paints and fill in berries with red glass paints. Dust with glitter. Let dry.

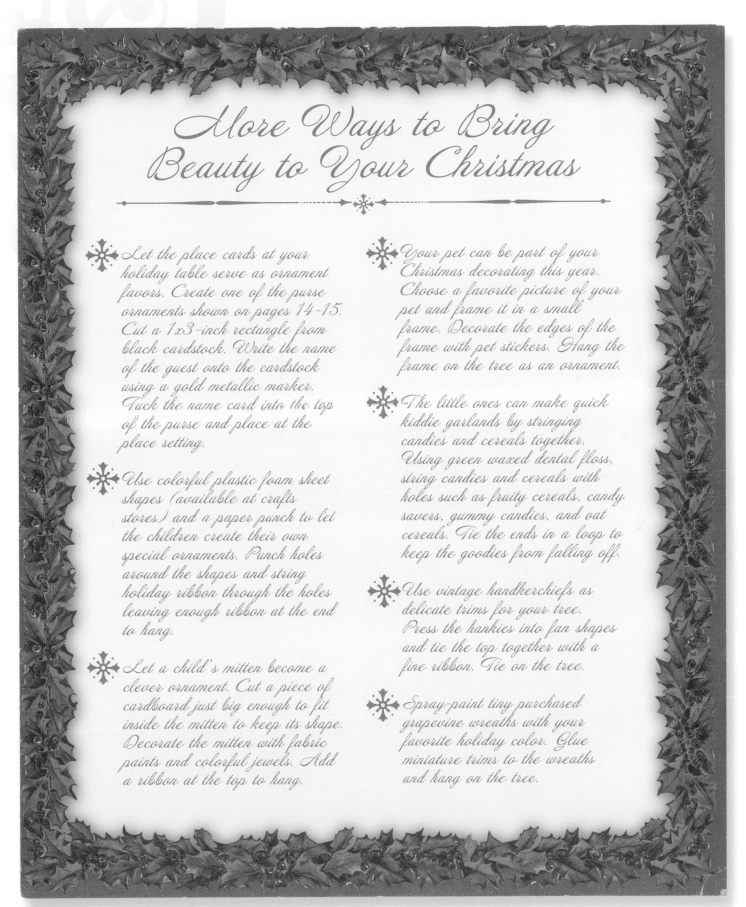

More Ways to Bring Beauty to Your Christmas

Let the place cards at your holiday table serve as ornament favors. Create one of the purse ornaments shown on pages 14-15. Cut a 1x3-inch rectangle from black cardstock. Write the name of the guest onto the cardstock using a gold metallic marker. Tuck the name card into the top of the purse and place at the place setting.

Use colorful plastic foam sheet shapes (available at crafts stores) and a paper punch to let the children create their own special ornaments. Punch holes around the shapes and string holiday ribbon through the holes leaving enough ribbon at the end to hang.

Let a child's mitten become a clever ornament. Cut a piece of cardboard just big enough to fit inside the mitten to keep its shape. Decorate the mitten with fabric paints and colorful jewels. Add a ribbon at the top to hang.

Your pet can be part of your Christmas decorating this year. Choose a favorite picture of your pet and frame it in a small frame. Decorate the edges of the frame with pet stickers. Hang the frame on the tree as an ornament.

The little ones can make quick kiddie garlands by stringing candies and cereals together. Using green waxed dental floss, string candies and cereals with holes such as fruity cereals, candy savers, gummy candies, and oat cereals. Tie the ends in a loop to keep the goodies from falling off.

Use vintage handkerchiefs as delicate trims for your tree. Press the hankies into fan shapes and tie the top together with a fine ribbon. Tie on the tree.

Spray-paint tiny purchased grapevine wreaths with your favorite holiday color. Glue miniature trims to the wreaths and hang on the tree.

Beautifully

sewn

tinseled

collected

arranged

ribboned

stamped

snowed

glittered

Holiday Decorations and Stunning Displays

Set the mood this holiday season with decorating ideas that are sure to reflect this most happy time of year. Create a beautiful wreath with colorful glass, sew a striped satin Christmas stocking, tie a polka-dot bow on the banister, or add jingle bells to your outside lights. Whatever you do, add a personal touch to your holiday decorating and your home will sparkle with the season.

SNOWFLAKE STAMPED LAMPSHADE

Make your light shine with a clever lampshade beautifully gilded for the holidays.

What you do:

Plan the design on the lampshade by following a pattern on the shade or mark with a pencil where the stamps will be placed. Hold the paper towel behind the shade and print the motifs on the shade, randomly changing the motif and ink pad color. Let the lampshade dry overnight before using.

So Easy

Stamping on a lampshade is easy because the fabric accepts the ink very well. And because the shade is already propped on the stand, you can work on all sides at once. You can make a clever lampshade in less than an hour!

POLISHED GLASS WREATH

Pieces of glass, polished to an elegant sparkle, overlap to make this striking holiday welcoming wreath.

What you do:

Spray paint the wreath form red. Let dry. Pour the bag of glass pieces into a dish or on a table. Pick out the pieces needed and plan the arrangement on the wreath. Glue the pieces to the form, overlapping the pieces as necessary to make the desired arrangement. Work on the front of the wreath first and allow to dry. Cover the edges of the foam, both inside and out. Allow to dry. Glue or wire a bow and evergreen trim at the top.

What you need:
- **Red spray paint**
- **One bag of polished glass pieces in assorted colors (available at crafts stores)**
- **Plastic foam wreath form**
- **Tacky crafts glue**
- **Striped ribbon**
- **Wire; evergreen**

Bring the magic of Christmas to the outside of your home with these three outdoor lighting ideas.

Trim outside lanterns with bows and simple embellishments. If the lantern is rustic in appearance, try a Pinecone and Feather Trim to adorn the light. Add a printed ribbon bow. Gold edged wide ribbon and gold jingle bells strung on smaller coordinating ribbon combine to trim the Holiday Red Lantern. The All-in-Blue Trim, has a vintage brooch pinned to the bow and is finished off with a string of cut, shiny blue beads.

42

Lanterns

So Easy Each of these outdoor lanterns was trimmed in just a few minutes. Tie the bows first and then wire the embellishments to the bows leaving enough wire at the ends to attach the bow arrangement to the lantern. You'll have showy outdoor holiday lights in no time!

ALL IN GREEN WREATH

Welcome your holiday guests with this beautiful green wreath, dusted in glitter and topped off with a happy polka-dot bow and a retro paper tree.

What you do:

Loop the wire around the wreath form, twisting it at the top, before starting to add the greens. Leave plenty of wire for hanging and twist together for a hanger. Choose desired holiday artificial greens. We chose greens that were lime green in color, and spray painted others to mix and match when necessary. Break or cut off pieces of the greens and poke them into the foam wreath form. Pull them out and glue in with strong crafts glue. Continue until the entire wreath is covered. Let the glue dry. Cut off small bunches of grapes and glue into greens. Using the large paint brush, lightly brush the glue and water mixture over the greens; dust with glitter. Let dry.

Lay the two ribbons atop each other and tie into a bow. Wire the bow onto the wreath. Color copy the tree pattern, *below*, onto cardstock and cut out. Poke tiny holes where desired and add a tiny colored brad in each hole. Add the sticker star to the top of the tree. Place the tree in the center of the wreath and glue in place. Allow to dry.

tree pattern

What you need:

- Purchased 9-inch green oasis foam wreath form
- Fine copper wire for hanging
- Purchased artificial holiday greens such as stems of evergreen, eucalyptus, holly, etc.
- Artificial green grapes
- Strong crafts glue such as E6000
- Lime green spray paint (optional)
- Glue and water mixture (2 tablespoons water and 2 tablespoons white crafts glue)
- Large paintbrush
- Green glitter
- Artificial red berries (optional)
- 1 yard of 2-inch wide polka dot grosgrain ribbon
- 1 yard of 2-inch wide green wire-edged ribbon
- Scissors
- Paper tree pattern
- Small colored brads (available at scrapbooking and crafts stores)
- Small star sticker

Clever Ornament Displays

There is always a place to gather together favorite ornaments.
Group your favorite golden ornaments together on a gold-trimmed
dish to create a Golden Display. If you are lucky enough to have some
vintage boxes in your collection, open up the box and fill it with all
colors of tiny ornaments in various shapes to make a Vintage Box of
Trims. Whatever your favorite color palette might be, let it guide you
to fill clear or colored glass containers with shades of these favorite
hues. Choose a grouping of three glass dishes such as lemon
reamers, pitchers, or small vases to create Colorful Trios.

Find that box of wonderful ornaments and display them in places other than on the tree! Look for dishes in the cupboard or places in your home to show off these wonderful trims.

What you need:

- Tracing paper
- Pencil
- Scissors
- Pinking shears
- ½ yard each of yellow and purple satin
- ½ yard of iron-on fleece
- 1 yard of red satin
- Red sewing thread
- 4 red jingle bells (18 mm)

48

COLORFUL JESTER STOCKING

Stripes of satin and bright red jingle bells combine to make this stocking a happy addition to Christmastime decorating.

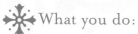 What you do:

Enlarge and trace stocking and cuff patterns, *below.* Cut out patterns. Cut two stocking pieces from iron-on fleece. From red satin, cut two stocking lining pieces. From red satin, cut two cuff pieces from pattern, placing side on fold, adding ¼-inch seam allowances on all other edges. Set aside. Using pinking shears, cut yellow, purple, and red satin into strips measuring 14-inches long and varying in widths from 1 to 3 inches. Piece together in desired order, enough strips to equal two pieces of pieced fabric approximately 14x21 inches each. Cut stocking front and back from pieced fabric, adding ¼-inch seam allowances to all sides. Cut a 1x8-inch piece of red satin for hanging loop. Iron fleece onto the back of front and back stocking pieces. Sew right sides together, using ¼-inch seams and leaving top edges free. Clip curves, turn, and press. With right sides together, sew lining stocking pieces together using ¼-inch seams. Clip seams. With right sides together, fold long sides of loop together and stitch, leaving short edges free. Turn right side out and press.

Insert lining inside stocking. Pin loop at side of stocking, having cut edges even with top unfinished edges of stocking and lining, with loop extending downward.

Sew cuff pieces with right sides together, leaving long top edge open. Trim across bottom of points and clip carefully into inside points before turning and pressing. Insert cuff inside stocking with top raw edges even and side sewn edges at side seam with hanger. Sew a ⅜-inch seam around top of stocking, joining cuff to top. Overcast edges. Flip cuff over stocking to front.

Handsew jingle bells to toe and cuff points.

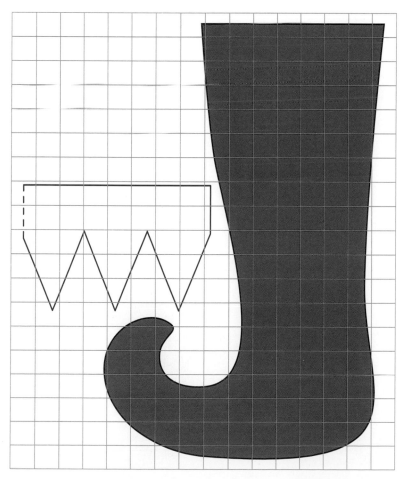

1 square = 1 inch   **enlarge 400%**

BELL-TRIMMED CHENILLE WREATH

This 10-inch wreath is trimmed with a single bell ornament and curly ribbon.

✤ **What you need:**

- **12x29-inch piece of chenille fabric cut across the grain with dark and light green colors (available at crafts stores or flea market stores)**
- **Matching color polyester thread; needle**
- **Polyfil stuffing**
- **Long stick such as a chopstick**
- **Straight pins**
- **Bell ornament**
- **1 yard of ³/₈-inch wide wire edge green ribbon**

✤ What you do:

With right sides together, sew short ends of rectangle together using ³/₈-inch seam. Turn. Take the top raw edge and fold down inside the tube putting raw edges together. With wrong sides together, stitch and overcast long edges together, leaving two inches open to stuff. Do not turn. Stuff circular tube, working polyfil around with a long stick to shape tube. Make sure long seam is at center back of wreath. With pins, mark five even places around wreath to indicate where to cinch in tube. With a double thread, take a few stitches in bottom seam at one pin marking. Loop the long threads over and around the tube 2 to 3 times to pull in fabric tightly. Anchor by taking three stitches in the bottom seam; tie off to secure. Repeat at each remaining marking. Make a bow and tie to top of wreath. Cut another 10-inch piece of ribbon and put bell on ribbon. Knot to secure. Tie into the bow at the top of the wreath.

To Give

✤ *If you have some chenille from a worn bedspread that has some family history, make a wreath for each of your sisters or brothers. What a joy to bring out the wreath every year and remember the fabrics of years ago.*

50

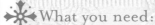
FLOWER TRIMMED CHENILLE WREATH

This large 12-inch wreath is trimmed with a matching chenille flower.

❋ What you do:

Construct the basic wreath as for Bell-Trimmed Chenille Wreath, on *page 50. For flower and leaf embellishments,* cut flowers and leaves from chenille fabric, leaving ¹/₄-inch around edges for seam. Cut plain cotton fabric for backing to same size. Cut iron-on fleece to same size as flower and leaf shapes and iron onto backsides of shapes. With right sides together, stitch shapes to backing fabric pieces, leaving an opening to turn. Clip seam allowance around curves and points. Turn right sides out and handstitch opening closed. Tack shapes to wreath sewing a few stitches, as needed, to secure in place.

So Easy

❋ What you need:

- 10x27-inch piece of soft green chenille fabric cut across the grain
- Polyfil stuffing
- Matching color polyester thread; needle
- Purchased white bottle brush trees (available at gift and crafts stores)
- Strands of pearls (new from crafts stores or vintage)
- Hot glue and glue sticks

TREE-TRIMMED CHENILLE WREATH

This 8-inch wreath is simply decorated with white bottle brush trees and strands of pearls.

❋ What you do:

Construct the basic wreath as for the Bell-Trimmed Chenille Wreath on *page 50*. Cover each of the five cinched-in areas with strands of pearls. Take a few stitches in the back of the wreath using matching thread to secure. Adjust as necessary.

Loop other strands of pearls together as desired. Secure in the center of the wreath by sewing with a few stitches. Place the bottle brush trees in the center of the wreath over the pearls. Glue to secure using hot glue. Allow to dry.

CHENILLE WREATH ORNAMENTS

Tiny and soft, these sweet little wreaths are dressed up with some pretty pearls for the holidays. The small groupings of three pearls look like tiny holly berries.

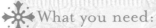

What you need:
- 9½x3-inch piece of soft green chenille fabric, cut across the grain
- Polyfil stuffing
- Matching color polyester thread
- Small tool such as a nutpick
- Needle
- Pearls on a string (new from crafts stores or vintage)
- Strong crafts glue
- Toothpick

What you do:

Construct the basic wreath as for the Bell-Trimmed Wreath on *page 50*. Because the ornaments are smaller, use a nut pick or small stick to push the polyfil into the tube.

To add the pearls, cut the pearls from the string or cut string and collect pearls in a small container. Arrange each set of pearls on the ornament at each area where the wreath was cinched in. Using the toothpick, make three dots with the glue. Place a pearl on each dot of glue. Allow to dry.

To hang, cut two 14-inch strands of pearls. Slip them through the center of the wreath and knot just above the wreath. Knot again about 2-inches above the first knot and hang on the tree.

53

Jolly Banisters

A pretty spot such as a stairway banister or newel post deserves its own special Christmas trim.

Make your banister the center of attention this holiday. The Nature Banister is decorated with greens, dried blooms, bird ornaments and a printed ribbon. The Kitchen Newel Post is adorned with a bright red ribbon, vintage cookie cutters, a candy cane, and a sprig of green. Our Sweet Polka-dot Trim is simply done by overlapping two ribbons and tying on some colorful rock candy to the newel post.

Family Affair

✳ Let the whole family get in on the decorating this year. A visit to the candy store brings home just the right candy trims and picking out ribbon at the discount or crafts store is fun for everyone.

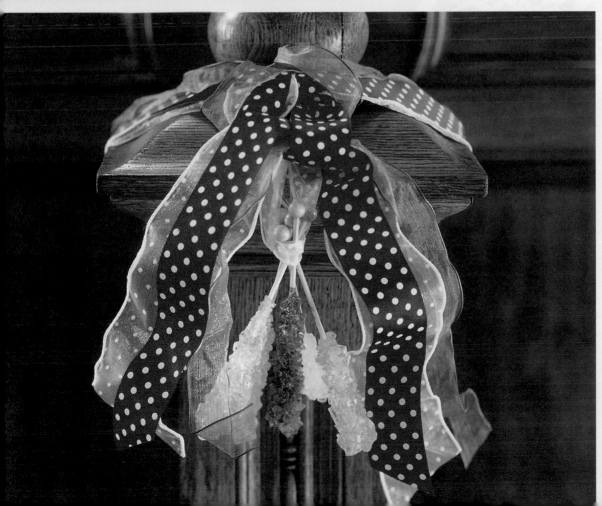

FANCY FUR-TOPPED STOCKING

So stylish with a faux fur cuff and black-satin stripes, this holiday stocking is meant for someone with real flair.

What you need:
- **Tracing paper**
- **Pencil**
- **½ yard of black stripe satin**
- **½ yard of black lining fabric**
- **¼ yard of black fake fur**
- **½ yard of iron-on fleece**
- **14 inches of black cording**
- **Black charm**
- **Thread to match fabrics**

What you do:

Enlarge and trace the patterns, *below,* onto tracing paper and cut out. Cut two stocking pattern pieces from black satin adding a ¼-inch seam allowance and two stocking patterns from lining fabric adding a ¼-inch seam allowance. Cut two stocking pieces from iron-on fleece. Place cuff pattern on fold of black fur and cut two pattern pieces.

Iron the fleece onto the back of stocking pieces. With right sides together, sew front to back with a ¼-inch seam, leaving top edges free. Clip curves, turn and press. With right sides together sew lining pieces together using a ¼-inch seam. Insert lining inside stocking. Cut an 8-inch piece of cording for hanger. Place cording at side of stocking, having cut edges even with top unfinished edges of stocking and lining, with loop extending downward.

Sew cuff pieces with right sides together, leaving long top edge open. Clip across corners diagonally. Turn and press. Insert cuff inside stocking with top raw edges even and side sewn edges at side seam with hanger. Sew ⅜-inch seam around top of stocking, joining cuff to top. Overcast edges. Flip cuff over stocking to front. Thread charm on remaining piece of cording. Tie the cording and charm under the cuff.

cuff pattern

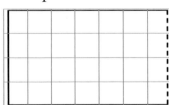

I square = I inch
enlarge 400%

stocking pattern

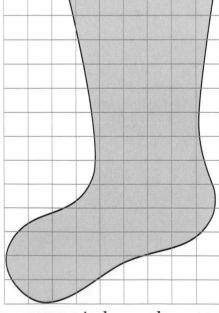

I square = I inch   enlarge 400%

WINTER WHITE STOCKING

Finished with an elegant vintage brooch, this stocking is made to fill with Christmas finery.

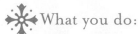What you do:

Enlarge and trace patterns, *below*, onto tracing paper and cut out. Cut two stocking patterns pieces from white satin adding ¼-inch allowance and two stocking patterns from lining fabrics adding ¼-inch seam allowance. Cut two stocking pieces from iron-on fleece. Place cuff pattern on fold of white satin and cut two cuff pattern pieces.

Iron fleece onto the back of stocking pieces. With right sides together, sew a ¼-inch seam, leaving top edges free. Clip curves, turn and press. With right sides together sew lining pieces together using a ¼-inch seam. Insert lining inside stocking. Pin cording at side of stocking, having cut edges even with top unfinished edges of stocking and lining, with loop extending downward.

Sew cuff pieces with right sides together, leaving long top edge open. Clip across corners diagonally. Turn and press. Insert cuff inside stocking with top raw edges even and side sewn edges of cuff at seam with hanger. Sew ⅜-inch seam around top of stocking, joining cuff to top. Overcast edges. Flip cuff over stocking to front. At loose side edge of cuff, gather up edge toward hanging loop and pin with a favorite brooch or pin to decorate.

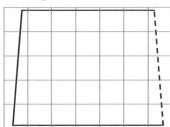

What you need:
- Tracing paper
- Pencil; scissors
- ½ yard of white print satin
- ½ yard of white lining fabric
- ½ yard of iron-on fleece
- 8 inches of white cording for hanger
- Thread to match fabrics
- Large vintage brooch-style pin

To Give

Make this gift as pure white as winter snow by filling it with things that are all white. White candy canes, a strand of pearls, white chocolate truffles, or a white milkglass cup and saucer are just the beginning of some all-white, much-loved gifts.

stocking pattern

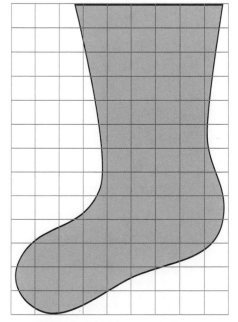

cuff pattern

I square = I inch
enlarge 400%

I square = I inch   enlarge 400%

ELEGANT TOPPER STAR

Use Christmas tree toppers to make this beautiful and unusual star to hang on your holiday door.

❊ What you do:

On the edge of the foam disc, mark five evenly-spaced dots. Use the knife to cut a hole at each dot just big enough for the base of the tree topper to fit into the hole. In a well ventilated area, spray paint the foam circle gold. Let dry. Glue the beads to the front of the foam disc. Glue the star on top of the beads. Place glue inside the holes and place toppers in the holes. Let dry. Push a hanger into the back of the foam for hanging.

Family Affair

❊*Holiday tree toppers can be found at crafts stores and discount stores where the ornaments are sold. Take the family along to pick out just the right colors, designs, and shapes to make this unique Christmas star.*

60

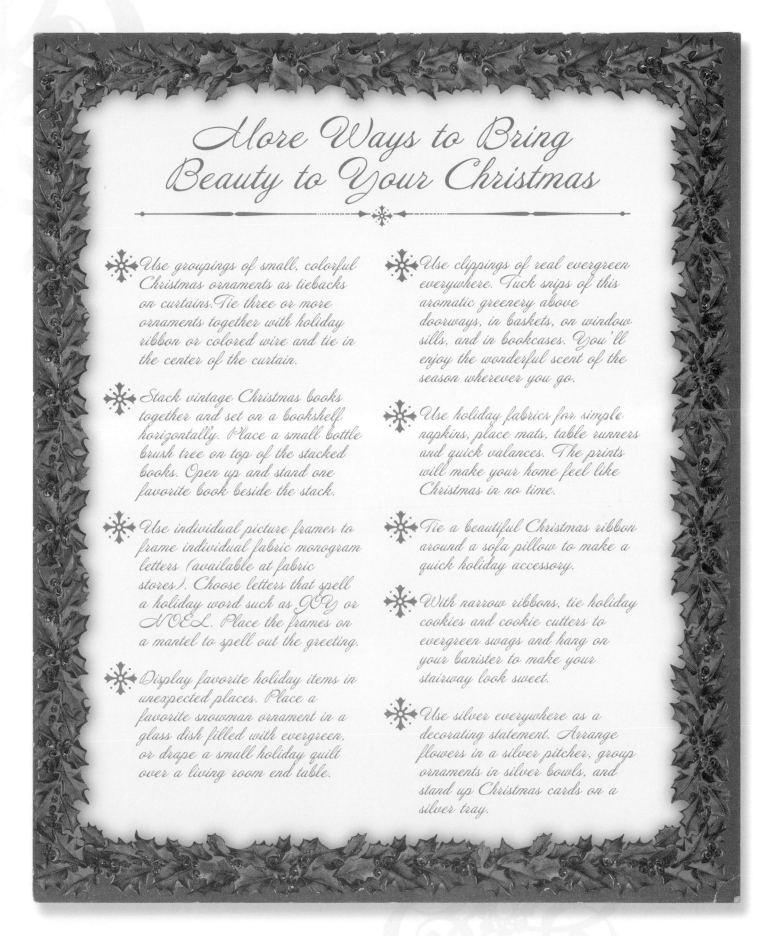

More Ways to Bring Beauty to Your Christmas

❄ Use groupings of small, colorful Christmas ornaments as tiebacks on curtains. Tie three or more ornaments together with holiday ribbon or colored wire and tie in the center of the curtain.

❄ Stack vintage Christmas books together and set on a bookshelf horizontally. Place a small bottle brush tree on top of the stacked books. Open up and stand one favorite book beside the stack.

❄ Use individual picture frames to frame individual fabric monogram letters (available at fabric stores). Choose letters that spell a holiday word such as JOY or NOEL. Place the frames on a mantel to spell out the greeting.

❄ Display favorite holiday items in unexpected places. Place a favorite snowman ornament in a glass dish filled with evergreen, or drape a small holiday quilt over a living room end table.

❄ Use clippings of real evergreen everywhere. Tuck snips of this aromatic greenery above doorways, in baskets, on window sills, and in bookcases. You'll enjoy the wonderful scent of the season wherever you go.

❄ Use holiday fabrics for simple napkins, place mats, table runners and quick valances. The prints will make your home feel like Christmas in no time.

❄ Tie a beautiful Christmas ribbon around a sofa pillow to make a quick holiday accessory.

❄ With narrow ribbons, tie holiday cookies and cookie cutters to evergreen swags and hang on your banister to make your stairway look sweet.

❄ Use silver everywhere as a decorating statement. Arrange flowers in a silver pitcher, group ornaments in silver bowls, and stand up Christmas cards on a silver tray.

Beautifully

ribboned

painted

folded

stitched

beaded

sewn

knitted

arranged

decorated

Clever Gifts and Unexpected Wraps

Handmade gifts are the dearest gifts of all. Whether you sew, knit, bead, or paint— whether you choose gifts and present them in a clever way, or wrap gifts and top them off with a handmade tag, you are giving of your talent to special friends and family. In this chapter you'll find ways to share the love of giving and experience the joy of creating for the ones you love.

HOLIDAY TIME

Make time more beautiful for a special friend with just a stroke of your hand and some pretty paint colors.

What you need:
- Purchased clock with wide smooth wood edge
- Pencil
- Acrylic paints in greens and white
- Paintbrush
- Small red jewels
- Tacky crafts glue

What you do:

Use the pencil to mark a small dot where you want the holly motifs to be painted. Using the photo, *below*, as a guide, paint the holly leaves by loading the brush with two colors of green and white. Paint the holly leaves on the clock rim and on the clock front. Allow to dry. Glue the red jewels on the leaves to resemble red berries.

❄ *Let the kids help find the holiday stickers at scrapbook and crafts stores—there are so many fun ones to pick from! And painting jar lids is a snap —even Dad will love to help make these projects!*

JAZZY JARS

Add a holiday sticker and a touch of pretty paint to a glass jar and fill it with goodies for a quick holiday give away.

❄ What you do:

We chose vintage jars with galvanized metal lids from an antiques store. New jar lids can be painted as well. Be sure the jar and lids are clean and dry. Choose the stickers before choosing the paint colors. Adhere the stickers to the jars. Paint the lids to coordinate with the stickers. Allow the paint to dry. Fill the jars with baking mixes or dried beans or other ingredients. Attach a recipe if desired. Put the lid on the top of the jar and add a ribbon and tag.

❄ What you need:
- **New or vintage glass jars**
- **Holiday stickers**
- **Paint (suitable for metal) to coordinate with stickers**
- **Paintbrush**
- **Ribbon to match stickers**

65

HOLIDAY KITCHEN SET

Stitch up this clever set and add a few baking accessories to make the perfect gift for the cook on your Christmas list.

What you do:

For the potholder, cut an 8-inch square *each* from red fabric and print fabric. Enlarge and trace potholder corner pattern, *below.* From pattern, cut four triangles, two from right side and two with pattern reversed. Cut two 8-inch squares from batting. Cut two triangles from batting.

Place layer of batting between triangle pieces, having right sides out. Baste around outside edges of both sections. Place two layers of batting between square pieces of fabric. With right sides out, baste around outside edges. Stitch bias tape to long angled edge of triangle pieces. Lay yarn at edge of bias tape and stitch over both. Position triangles over square piece and pin in place. On center plain fabric, between triangle pieces, mark line for swirling tree shape referring to swirl pattern, *below.* Using a darning foot and the same color of thread, zigzag stitch over green cording along marked line through all thicknesses of square piece. Apply binding to outside edges of square, starting at top of tree point and finishing at top with a loop to hang.

For the towel, trace tree outline onto bottom middle of kitchen towel. Zigzag stitch over length of cording over outline of tree shape. Cut strip of print fabric 1 ¼-inches wide and length of towel plus ½ inch. Turn in ¼ inch on each long side and iron to back. Place print strip over flat strip of towel, turning under ¼-inch at each side edge. Pin in place. Lay yarn at edges of strip and sew with decorative stitch to secure.

To present as a gift, place in baking pan with spatula, measuring spoons and cookie or cake mix. Wrap with ribbon.

potholder corner

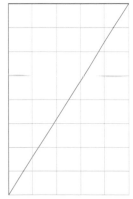

1 square = 1 inch

enlarge 400%

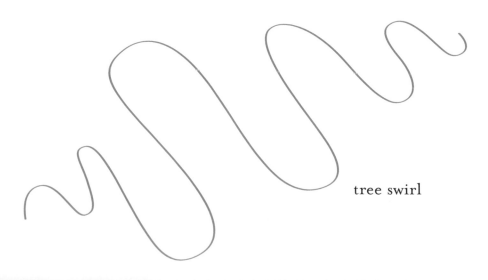

tree swirl

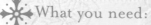

What you need:
- 6 pearls (5mm)
- 12 pearls (4mm)
- 12 multifaceted white glass beads (4mm)
- 10 pearls (3mm)
- 40-50 pearls (2mm or 8/0)
- 12 silver balls (3mm)
- 24 narrow silver spacers of choice
- 6 smoky gray crystals (3mm)
- ½-inch pearl button with shank
- 18 inches of pliable beading wire, such as C-Flex 49 strand, .012 clear beading wire
- 3 sterling silver crimp beads
- Masking tape

PEARL BUTTON BRACELET

The pearls are so lovely, but just look at the clever closure on this oh-so-pretty piece.

What you do:

Thread approximately 10-14 2mm pearls onto middle of wire. Bring both ends of wire together and string one crimp bead through both ends of wire simultaneously, forming a loop. Adjust loop so both ends of wire are even. Holding crimp bead tightly against the loop, check the fit of the loop by slipping the button through. Button should fit through easily. Adjust the fit; crimp bead by squeezing it firmly with pliers. Begin stringing beads on one piece of wire in the following pattern: 2mm pearl, spacer, faceted glass bead, spacer, 5mm pearl, spacer, faceted glass bead, spacer, silver ball, 2mm pearl, 2 (3mm) pearls, 3mm crystal, 2 (3mm) pearls, 2mm pearl, silver ball. Repeat pattern two more times, omitting the silver ball at end of the second repeat. Secure end of first wire with small piece of tape.

String the second wire in the following pattern: 3 (2mm) pearls, crystal, 3 (2mm) pearls, spacer, faceted bead, spacer, 5mm pearl, spacer, faceted bead, spacer, silver ball, 2mm pearl, 2 (3mm) pearls, 3mm crystal, 2 (3mm) pearls, 2mm pearl, silver ball, spacer, faceted bead, spacer, 5mm pearl, spacer, faceted bead, spacer, silver ball, 2mm pearl, 2 (3mm) pearls, 3mm crystal, 2 (3mm) pearls, 2mm pearl, silver ball, spacer, faceted bead, spacer, 5mm pearl, spacer, faceted bead, spacer, silver ball, 2 (2mm) pearls. Tape end of wire to secure ends. Wrap bracelet carefully around wrist to check fit. Adjust by adding or subtracting beads as necessary.

Finish the bracelet by removing tape from one wire and threading crimp bead on wire. Thread wire through shank of button and back through crimp bead and one more inch of beads. Pull any excess wire through to cinch beads closely. Repeat the procedure with other wire. Complete bracelet by crimping both beads. Cut off any excess wire from both strands.

CANDLE BRACELETS

Give these jeweled candle trims (that later become favorite bracelets) by stringing favorite beads onto elastic cording. Tie the ends securely and place around the glass votive holder for a clever two-in-one gift.

CHERRY CHARM NECKLACE

Make this charming cherry necklace for the sweetest person on your Christmas list.

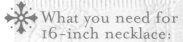

What you do:

Wrap a piece of tape at end of wire to keep beads from falling off. String a pattern of seed beads: 3 green, one red, 3 green. Then add one silver, one 4mm red, and one silver bead on wire. Repeat both patterns until you reach the tenth 4mm red bead. Do not add silver bead to complete pattern. String on one silver plated split ring and continue pattern, beginning with a red 4mm bead. Continue until there are nine red 4mm beads with corresponding seed bead pattern on either side of the two center 4mm beads. Be sure to end with the same seed bead pattern: 3 green, one red, 3 green.

Finish off the ends of the necklace by stringing one crimp bead at end of necklace, then one lobster claw. Bring wire back through crimp beads and also through approximately 1 inch of beads. There can be some excess wire sticking out from beads, but be sure to allow at least 1½ inches excess at opposite end to complete necklace. If there is not, adjust wire accordingly. Push crimp beads up snugly against lobster claw, making sure there is some play so that the claw can move freely. Crimp bead firmly with pliers.

Follow same procedure at other end of necklace using the split ring instead of lobster claw. Trim excess wire from either end of necklace as closely to beads as possible.

To make the charm, string one 5 mm red bead on headpin. Put headpin through split ring at middle of necklace. Bend pin to form loop and cross over one side of headpin with approximately ½-inch of wire with bead on it on first side of loop. String on leaf bead and other 5 mm red bead. Cut off excess wire from headpin, leaving about ¼ inch sticking out from second red bead. Using round nosed pliers, form a small loop tightly against red bead to secure it on headpin. Adjust the charms headpin wire with round nosed pliers, if necessary, so that it resembles two hanging cherries.

Wrap it Up!

Pretty ribbons, pretty fabrics, pretty paints—they all make wraps that make your gift one to remember.

Vintage sheet music makes a Clever Musical Wrap when you add a touch of glitter between the bars. Purchase a holiday silk scarf to create a Silk Presentation as you wrap it around the gift and secure it with a piece of gold cording. Little Painted Boxes become big hits when they are painted and dotted with the names of the lucky recipients.

So Easy

❄ *These ideas work best on small to medium size boxes and can all be done in a matter of minutes. The trick to writing the names on the purple boxes is to plan first by using a pencil to lightly mark the letters before starting to dot the names.*

73

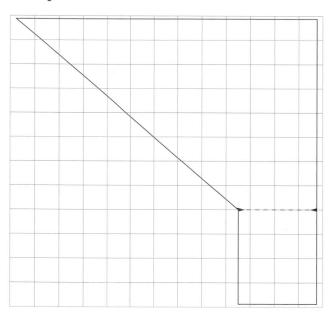

HAPPY SNOWMAN PILLOW

Complete with a fringed tassel, this happy fellow will bring a smile to all who see him.

❄ **What you need:**

- ¹/₂ yard of white fleece (for face)
- I yard colorful striped fleece
- Black and orange felt scraps for face details
- Embroidery floss
- 12-inch pillow form

❄ **What you do:**

Enlarge hat pattern, *below.* Trace all patterns onto tracing paper. Cut out. In addition, cut white fleece into a 12x12¹/₂-inch rectangle for face. Cut the striped fleece into the following shapes: One 3¹/₂x12¹/₂-inch piece (for scarf), one 3¹/₂x5¹/₂-inch piece (for scarf fringe), one 14x13 inch piece (for back) and one 10x¹/₂-inch piece (for hat tie). Cut two pieces from hat pattern. Using ¹/₄-inch seams and right sides together, sew long side of scarf piece to long side of white fleece forming a rectangle, placing striped fleece at bottom for scarf. The white becomes the face. Fold under one inch at top of white piece; stitch close to cut edge. Cut face shapes from felt; machine appliqué to face. Embroider mouth line using 3 strands of floss. *For the hat,* cut fringe by cutting every ¹/₂ inch up from bottom rectangle piece to notches on pattern. With right sides together, stitch straight side and the angled side from notches to top. Leave top open. Turn right side out. Stitch hat to back piece of fabric, placing hat on wrong side of back fabric, having straight edge to the right and angled edge to left. Hat piece should sit in ¹/₄-inch from each side edge. Add scarf fringe piece to front side of pillow by placing right side of fringe piece to wrong side of left bottom section of front piece, matching edges with scarf seam. With right sides together, stitch front to back, along side and bottom edges. Turn. Fringed piece should extend to the left and be enclosed in left seam. Fringe scarf by cutting in every ¹/₂ inch to a depth just before the side seam. Insert pillow form through top opening. Flip hat over top opening. Add hat tie and ornament trims if desired.

hat pattern

I square = I inch   enlarge 400%

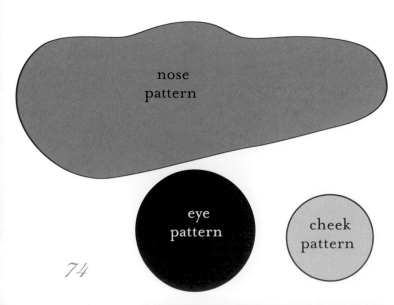

nose pattern

eye pattern

cheek pattern

So Easy

Make a colorful covered can wrap for everyone on your list. It is so easy to paint the can in whatever color matches the personality of the recipient. You can buy or make the magnets to decorate the pretty painted can.

What you need:

- **Tin can with lid (available at crafts and discount stores)**
- **Spray paints suitable for metal in two colors**
- **Small round ornament**
- **Small circle magnets**
- **Flat marbles in desired colors**
- **Strong crafts glue such as E6000**
- **Ribbon and tag**

MAGIC POLKA DOTS

This clever wrap is a gift in itself with some very magical qualities!

What you do:

Be sure the can is clean and dry. In a well-ventilated area, spray the lid of the can one color and the base another color. Set aside to dry. Remove the hanger part of the ornament. With the strong crafts glue, glue a magnet to the ornament top. Set aside to dry. Glue magnets to the flat sides of the marbles. Set aside to dry. Put the lid on the can. Place the magnet ornament on top of the can in the center. Add the magnets around the can in a polka-dot fashion. Tie a tag with gold ribbon and loop around the ornament top.

QUILT BLOCK WRAP

For the quilt lover on your list, make a package that is a quilter's dream and may even inspire a full size handmade quilt!

What you need:
- **Wrapped square flat-topped box in plain colored wrap**
- **Plain white paper**
- **Scrapbook papers in desired colors**
- **Scissors**
- **Adhesive such as glue stick**

What you do:

Measure the top of the box. Draw this measurement on the plain paper. Cut the scrapbook papers into squares and triangles. Practice making the design on the plain paper first.

Arrange the design on the top of the square wrapped package. Glue in place.

So Easy

❄ *Both of these easy-to-make pieces are worked on size 11 needles, so the projects go quickly. The look of time-consuming cables is mastered on the scarf with an easy to work pattern stitch and the cap features an easy lace stitch pattern with bobbles.*

❄ What you need:
- **Classic Elite, Bravo, 40% rayon/35% mohair/13% silk/6%wool/6% nylon, bulky weight yarn (48 yards per hank) 7 hanks of Red (3714)**
- **Size 11 (8.00mm) knitting needles or size needed to obtain gauge**
- **Yarn needle**

BOBBLE SCARF AND HAT

Who wouldn't love this handmade set of toasty warm winter gear. The soft mohair yarn and bobble stitch makes it fashion forward!

Skill Level: Easy

Size: Scarf is about 11x74 inches. Cap is 23 inches around and 8 inches tall.

Gauge: 12 sts and 13 rows = 4 inches/10cm.

TAKE TIME TO CHECK YOUR GAUGE.

Special Abbreviations:

Skp (slip, knit, pass over): Slip next stitch purlwise and with yarn on WS, knit next stitch, pass slipped stitch over the knit stitch — decrease made.

MB (make bobble): In next stitch (k1, yo, k1, yo, k1) to make 5 sts; turn, purl 5; turn, k3, k2tog, pass 3 sts, one at a time, over k2tog.

❄ What you do:

SCARF

Cast on 34 sts. Border: Purl 1 row, knit 1 row.

Row 3 (RS): (P2, yo, k3, skp, k9) twice, p2.

Row 4: (K2, p8, p2tog, p3, yo, p1) twice, k2.

Row 5: (P2, k2, yo, k3, skp, k7) twice, p2.

Row 6: (K2, p6, p2tog, p3, yo, p3) twice, k2.

Row 7: (P2, k4, yo, k3, skp, k5) twice, p2.

Row 8: (K2, p4, p2tog, p3, yo, p5) twice, k2.

Row 9: (P2, k6, yo, k3, skp, k3) twice, p2.

Row 10: (K2, p2, p2tog, p3, yo, p7) twice, k2.

Rep Rows 3-10 to approx 73" from beg, ending with a RS row. Border: Purl 1 row, knit 1 row. Bind off loosely and knitwise.

CAP

Beg at lower edge, cast on 71 sts. Border: Purl 1 row, knit 1 row.

Row 3: Knit.
Row 4: Purl.
Rows 5-6: As Rows 3-4.

Row 7: K1; * yo, skp, k1, k2tog, yo **, k5; rep from * across, ending last rep at **, k4.

Row 8 and each following WS row: Purl.

Row 9: K2; * yo, sl 1 st knitwise, k2tog, pass the slipped stitch over the k2tog, yo **, k7; rep from * across, ending last rep at **, k6.

Row 11: K3; * MB, k9; rep from * across, ending MB, k8.

Row 12: Purl.

Knit 1 row, dec 1 st. Purl 70 sts.

Crown Shaping

Row 1 (RS): K1; (k2tog, k8) 6 times, k2tog, k7.

Row 2: P63.

Row 3: K1; (k2tog, k7) 6 times, k2tog, k6.

Row 4: P56.

Row 5: K1; (k2tog, k6) 6 times, k2tog, k5.

Row 10: P49.

Row 11: K1; (k2tog, k5) 6 times, k2tog, k4.

Row 12: P42.

Row 13: K1; (k2tog, k4) 6 times, k2tog, k3.

Row 14: P35.

Row 15: K1; (k2tog, k3) 6 times, k2tog, k2.

Row 14: P28.

Row 15: (K2tog) across.

Row 16: P14.

Leaving a long tail, break yarn. Thread tail into yarn needle and back through rem sts. Pull up to close top. Sew the back seam.

PAINTED POINSETTIA GOBLETS

Painted with transparent glass paints, this beautiful pair of goblets will be treasured forever.

❄ What you do:

Be sure the goblets are clean and dry. Avoid touching the surface area to be painted. Pour a small amount of each color of paint onto the plate. Load the brush with the red, purple, and white paint all together. Starting from the inside of the flower, paint a stroke outward (see photo, *right*). Continue

painting these petals outward, reloading the brush as needed. The colors will mix as the paint is applied. Using a clean paintbrush, use yellow to make small dots in the center of the flower. Allow to dry. Air dry or bake following the manufacturer's instructions.

SO SWEET
What could be sweeter than a treasure hidden in pink sugar? The holder of this purchased jewelry is a striped candy cup purchased at a candy store. Fill the cup with coarse pastel-colored sugar and tuck in the jewelry for a sweet surprise.

81

For the Soup Lover, give the bowls and spoons as well as the soup mix. Tie it all together with a holiday bow. For the Master Cook, present a collection of cooking items that are sure to please. Fill a utensil holder with color-coordinated kitchen items, fun-colored sugars, and specialty chocolates. For the Talented Artist, decorate the top of a purchased jewelry box with your own artwork. Fill the box with new paint brushes and colorful tubes of paint.

Family Affair

❄ *Go to the store as a family to pick out the items you need to make perfect gifts for everyone on your Christmas list. Give everyone in the family one person to shop for and then gather together to see what surprises you all have found.*

So easy to make and so fun to give, the mittens in this fleece set of winter wear are tucked away in a jar.

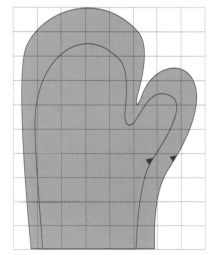

What you need:

- **Tracing paper**
- **1 yard of 45-inch-wide fleece**
- **³/₈-inch wide clear elastic—for small, 12 inches of elastic (two 6-inch pieces)—for large, 18 inches of elastic (two 9-inch pieces)**
- **Matching thread**
- **Pinking shears**

For the wrap:

- **Snow Fun Art on pages 156-157**
- **Scissors**
- **Canning jar**
- **Curly ribbon**

What you do:

For mittens, enlarge desired pattern, *below,* onto tracing paper. Cut out. Use pinking shears to cut 4 mitten patterns, placing stretch to go around hand. Using ¹/₄-inch seams and right sides together, sew two mitten pieces together from notch to bottom edge. Open up mitten. On the wrong side, mark a line for elastic placement, 2 ¹/₂ inches up from bottom edge. Cut elastic to length needed leaving 1-inch from end to hold on to under presser foot to make it easier to stretch across the mitten. Stretching elastic, zigzag over the elastic and sew in place. With right sides together, sew mitten from notch around to lower edge, matching elastic marks. Repeat for other mitten. Turn right side out. *For scarf,* cut fleece into a rectangle 8¹/₂-inches wide and 45 inches long. Use pinking shears to cut fringe on each end of fleece cutting every ¹/₂ inch in to a depth of 3 inches. *For the Mitten Wrap,* cut out desired art and use as tags and jar inset. Roll mittens and put in jar. Tie tags on with curly ribbon.

mitten patterns

I square = I inch

enlarge 400%

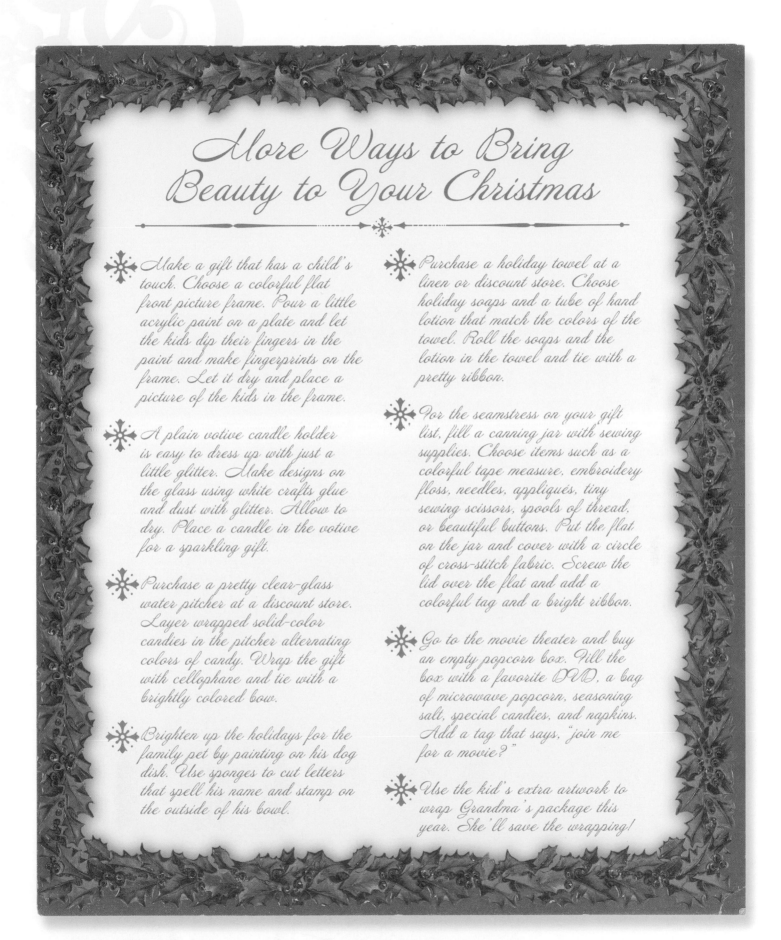

More Ways to Bring Beauty to Your Christmas

❄ Make a gift that has a child's touch. Choose a colorful flat front picture frame. Pour a little acrylic paint on a plate and let the kids dip their fingers in the paint and make fingerprints on the frame. Let it dry and place a picture of the kids in the frame.

❄ A plain votive candle holder is easy to dress up with just a little glitter. Make designs on the glass using white crafts glue and dust with glitter. Allow to dry. Place a candle in the votive for a sparkling gift.

❄ Purchase a pretty clear-glass water pitcher at a discount store. Layer wrapped solid-color candies in the pitcher alternating colors of candy. Wrap the gift with cellophane and tie with a brightly colored bow.

❄ Brighten up the holidays for the family pet by painting on his dog dish. Use sponges to cut letters that spell his name and stamp on the outside of his bowl.

❄ Purchase a holiday towel at a linen or discount store. Choose holiday soaps and a tube of hand lotion that match the colors of the towel. Roll the soaps and the lotion in the towel and tie with a pretty ribbon.

❄ For the seamstress on your gift list, fill a canning jar with sewing supplies. Choose items such as a colorful tape measure, embroidery floss, needles, appliqués, tiny sewing scissors, spools of thread, or beautiful buttons. Put the flat on the jar and cover with a circle of cross-stitch fabric. Screw the lid over the flat and add a colorful tag and a bright ribbon.

❄ Go to the movie theater and buy an empty popcorn box. Fill the box with a favorite DVD, a bag of microwave popcorn, seasoning salt, special candies, and napkins. Add a tag that says, "join me for a movie?"

❄ Use the kid's extra artwork to wrap Grandma's package this year. She'll save the wrapping!

Beautifully
painted
glittered
carved
decoupaged
sewn
felted
jeweled
decorated

Table Trims and Welcoming Centerpieces

Friends gather, family comes from far away–the holidays are here and it is time for entertaining. In this chapter you'll find ideas that are simple to make yet look stunning on your table. You'll find centerpieces that sparkle and place cards that will make you smile. You'll find cozy holders for utensils and snowman favors that jingle. Enjoy your time together as you entertain in style.

Let your table reflect the light of the season with these easy-to-make, colorful candle holders.

❊ **What you need:**
- **Tissue paper**
- **Scissors–straight edge, pinking, or scalloped edge**
- **White glue; water**
- **Small glass jar**
- **Small paintbrush**
- **Wax paper**
- **Clear acrylic spray**
- **Glitter and ribbon (optional)**
- **Tea light candles**

❊ What you do:

Tear or cut tissue paper into small pieces about 1-inch square. Use decorative scissors if desired. Make a mixture of 2 tablespoons glue and 2 tablespoons water. Use the paintbrush to coat a small area of the jar with a thin layer of diluted glue. Lightly press on tissue paper (either flat or crinkled for a more textured look). Brush a thin layer of the glue mixture over all of the edges and the top, covering the entire jar (see photos, *below*). Dust with glitter if desired. Place onto waxed paper to dry. Seal with acrylic spray when finished. Add a ribbon at the top if desired. When dry, insert tea light candle. Never leave a burning candle unattended.

Family Affair

❊ *Let the kids help cut the pieces of paper. The shapes do not have to be cut the same—the colors will blend and look more beautiful with more hands to help.*

TINY CANDLE CHARMS

Candy canes, tiny stars and sparkling trees charm even the most stately candle.

What you do:

Trace patterns, *below*, onto tracing paper and cut out. Roll each color of clay to ⅛-inch thickness. Draw around patterns onto desired color of clay. Cut out. (Use decorative-edge scissors if desired.) Lay all pieces on baking sheet. With toothpick, poke four holes in opposite sides of each flat piece and in top of trees and stars. Make candy canes by rolling white and red clay together into a rope about ¼-inch thick. Cut into 2-inch lengths and bend the tops. Make four canes. Cut paper clip ends off using wire cutters. Insert into tops of candy canes. Lay on baking sheet with other pieces. Bake as directed by manufacturer. Cool. Apply a thin coat of glue to tops of large pieces, stars, and trees. Dust with glitter. Connect small pieces to large pieces using fine wire. Place on candlestick. Place candle in holder.

What you need:
- Tracing paper
- Polymer clay such as Sculpey in red, silver, white, and dark green
- Rolling pin
- Knife
- Scissors
- Decorative edge scissors
- Toothpick
- Small paper clips
- Wire cutters
- Crafts glue
- Fine glitter in green and silver
- Fine wire

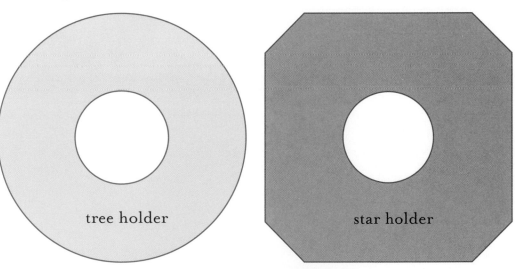

tree holder

star holder

tree pattern
cut 4

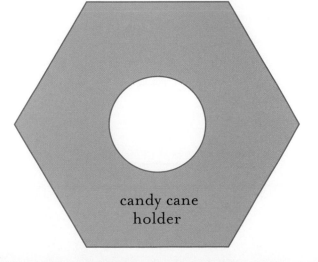

candy cane
holder

star pattern
cut 4

To Give

❄ *Make this candle a special gift by placing it in a box with other ornaments of the same color. What a surprise to find a unique candle in the shape of an ornament!*

❄ **What you need:**
- **Round ball candle (available at crafts and discount stores)**
- **Waxed paper**
- **Linoleum cutter and blade**
- **Soft cloth**
- **Gold acrylic paint**
- **Large paintbrush**
- **Purchased large round Christmas ornament with gold top**
- **Small plate**
- **Small ornaments**

CARVED ORNAMENT CANDLE
Create your own piece of carved art to grace your holiday table by creating this clever candle.

❄ **What you do:**

Decide on a simple design to carve into the candle. Some candles have color only on the outside so carving reveals a white wax underneath. Place the candle on the waxed paper. Carving away from hands and face, carve the design into the wax. Do not push too hard or deep into the wax. The wax should carve easily. When finished, wipe the candle with a soft rag to remove any small pieces of wax. Brush the candle with the paint. Immediately wipe off paint with the rag, leaving just a little gold paint. Remove the top of the purchased Christmas ornament. Remove the hanger from the top. Turn it upside down and push into the candle. Set the candle on a plate and surround with small ornaments. Never leave a burning candle unattended.

COZY SPOON HOLDER
Make holiday suppers even warmer with these simple spoon holders created with brightly colored felt.

❋ What you do:

Enlarge and trace stocking pattern, *right*, onto tracing paper. Place pattern on felt and cut two stocking shapes from pattern using pinking shears. Insert cording at top heel edge forming a loop. Baste in place. Stitch around the stocking close to the edges, leaving the top open. Backstitch at the start and at the end to reinforce cording loop. Add stickers to finished stocking, gluing if necessary to adhere.

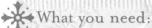

❋ What you need:
- Tracing paper
- Two 4x8-inch pieces of brightly colored felt
- Variegated sewing thread
- Pinking shears
- 4-inch piece of $^1/_4$-inch wide cording in color to match felt
- Star stickers
- Glue, optional

stocking pattern

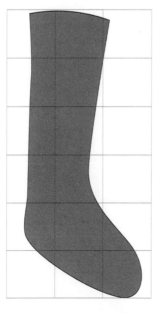

I square = I inch

enlarge 200%

Every guest will easily find their place when they come to dine this Christmas season. Their initial, so beautifully embellished with jewels and charms, will be a clue where to sit and enjoy the holiday meal.

✸ **What you need:**
- **Purchased wood letter that can stand alone (available at craft and discount stores)**
- **Acrylic paint in desired color**
- **Paintbrushes**
- **White crafts glue**
- **Vintage jewelry**
- **Purchased crafting jewels and beads**
- **Small rick rack or lace trims**
- **Micro-mini beads in desired color**
- **Disposable plate**

✸ **What you do:**

Paint the wood letter the desired color. Let the paint dry. Starting at one corner, arrange the jewelry, beads, and other trims as desired and glue to the letter working on one area at a time. After the jewels are in place, use a paintbrush to paint glue in the open areas. Place the letter over a disposable plate and cover with micro-mini beads working on one side at a time until the letter and edges are completely covered. Let dry.

To Give

✸ *Make the beautiful embellished letter a gift by placing it in a small box and wrapping it with paper that has been stamped with the initials of the receiver. Tie an elegant bow around the box and present it for a treasured gift.*

CANDLE TABLE FAVOR

Use press-on rhinestone jewels to spell the name of this honored guest and place a candle in the center to make a warm table greeting.

What you do:

Remove the top of the ornament and discard the hanger part. Use an awl to make a hole in the metal topper just big enough for the candle. Set aside. Fill the ornament with rice until it will sit level and not fall over. Press on the rhinestone letters spelling the name of the guest. Replace the metal topper. Place a candle in the hole of the topper. Set the ornament on a small plate. Never leave a burning candle unattended.

What you need:
- **Ornament in desired color**
- **Awl**
- **1/2 cup dry rice**
- **Press-on rhinestone letters**
- **Silver birthday candle**
- **Small glass plate**

Napkin Trims

Make it a white Christmas by choosing a white tassel, snowflake, and ribbon to create a Winter White Napkin Tie. Two striped ornaments combine with striped candy sticks to make this Colorful Tie Up for the holidays. A vintage brooch and handkerchief are pinned together to make our Memorable Holiday Napkin.

To Give

❄ Let the lucky guest keep their napkin holder as a gift. The pretty snowflake can be used to hang in a window, the colorful striped ornaments can hang on the tree, and the lovely vintage brooch can be worn as it once was during the holiday season.

So Easy

Because the art is already done for you, all you need to do is color copy, cut out, and decoupage the circles to the coaster shapes. You can make multiple sets of these coordinating coaster designs in an evening.

What you need:
- **Art from page 154**
- **Purchased round wooden coaster or wooden 4-inch disc**
- **Red cording**
- **Decoupage medium**
- **Paintbrush**
- **White crafts glue**

ARTFUL COASTERS

A beautiful addition to any holiday table, these artful coasters make a wonderful table favor.

What you do:

Color copy or scan the art on *page 154* reducing it by 75%. Print the art onto cardstock. Cut out. Paint a coat of decoupage medium onto the wood disc or coaster. Lay the cut paper art on top and paint a coat of decoupage medium over the paper. Let dry about an hour. Add two more layers of decoupage medium over the coasters letting the coasters dry thoroughly between coats. Cut a piece of red cording just long enough to fit around the edge of the coaster. Glue in place with crafts glue. Paint one more layer of decoupage medium over the entire coaster and cording. Allow to dry.

PURPLE POINSETTIA CANDLE RING

So rich and elegant, these pretty purple poinsettias and grapes make a lovely centerpiece.

What you do:

In a well ventilated area, lay the string of poinsettias and the foam wreath on the newspaper and spray with one shade of the purple paint. Let dry. Lightly spray the poinsettias again using the other color of purple paint, letting the first color show through. Allow to dry. Lay the poinsettias on the wreath and pin in place. Cut off more poinsettias from the remaining yard and pin in place to fill wreath. Glue the grapes in place between the poinsettias. Lay on the table and add a pillar candle in the middle. Never leave a burning candle unattended.

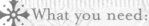What you need:

- **1 yard of artificial poinsettias**
- **Two colors of purple spray paint**
- **9-inch foam wreath, such as Styrofoam**
- **Artificial sugared purple grapes**
- **Long pins**
- **Hot glue gun and glue sticks**
- **Purple pillar candle**

SANTA PLACE SET

Welcome your guests with Santa holding each name card and a matching napkin ring.

What you need:
- Santa and Border Art from page 153
- Small scissors
- Crafts glue
- 1x3-inch piece of natural-colored cardstock
- 1x6-inch piece of white cardstock for stand
- Paper punch
- Gold ribbon

What you do:

For the Santa name card, scan or color copy the Country Santa Art on *page 153*. Cut out around the Santa shape referring to the photo, *opposite.* Using a computer font, spell the name of the guest and print out on cream paper. Glue to the front section of the Santa cut out. Fold the white cardstock in half, creating a stand. Glue to the back. *For the napkin ring,* scan or color copy the Holiday Border Art, *page 153*. Cut to desired length. Punch a hole in each end and thread the gold ribbon through the holes. Tie around the napkin.

SWEET CENTERPIECE

Create this clever arrangement by choosing two vases that fit inside each other. Arrange jelly beans between the glass vases. Add water to the inside vase and add fresh roses and greens.

YULE LOG CANDLES

Tiny tea lights nestle inside natural logs to make a warm and rustic glow.

What you need:

❄ • Pieces of 3 or 4-inch diameter wood cut into lengths of 3 to 6 inches
• Drill and 1½-inch drill bit
• Tea lights in metal cups

❄ What you do:

Cut the logs into different heights. Be sure the logs are cut straight and will stand up securely and remain level. Put the logs into a vice. Using the 1½-inch drill bit, drill into the log, drilling about 1 inch deep into the wood. Be sure the hole is level. Clean out any sawdust. Check to be sure the log will sit upright without tipping over. Place the tea candle in its metal holder into the hole making sure the metal surrounds the entire candle. *Note:* Tea lights burn quickly. Never leave a candle unattended.

STRIPED SAND CANDLES

Choose square glass candle holders and layer colorful sand that matches your holiday decor. Nestle a votive candle in the sand and surround the holders with nature trims to make the look complete.

JOLLY JINGLE TABLE FAVOR

So happy to greet your guests, this happy snowman almost becomes part of the family.

What you do:

Using a piece of clay about the size of a golf ball, shape the snowman head and hat on the top of the bell. Make a tiny carrot nose and attach to the face. Use the rolling pin to roll out a piece of clay ¼-inch thick, about ½ inch wide, and 3 inches long. Wrap this piece around the base of the head. Use scissors to fringe the scarf edge. Allow the clay to air-dry on the bell overnight. The clay will shrink slightly. When dry, add glue where necessary to attach to bell. Use markers to make dots for the eyes and mouth and to color the nose. Add a thin layer of glue to the scarf and hat. Dust with silver glitter. Allow to dry.

To Give

This clever fellow can serve as a wonderful ornament as well as a napkin tie—perfect for the snowman-lover on your list. Lay the finished ornament in a small box filled with white tinsel garland. Wrap the box with snowman wrapping paper and a white bow.

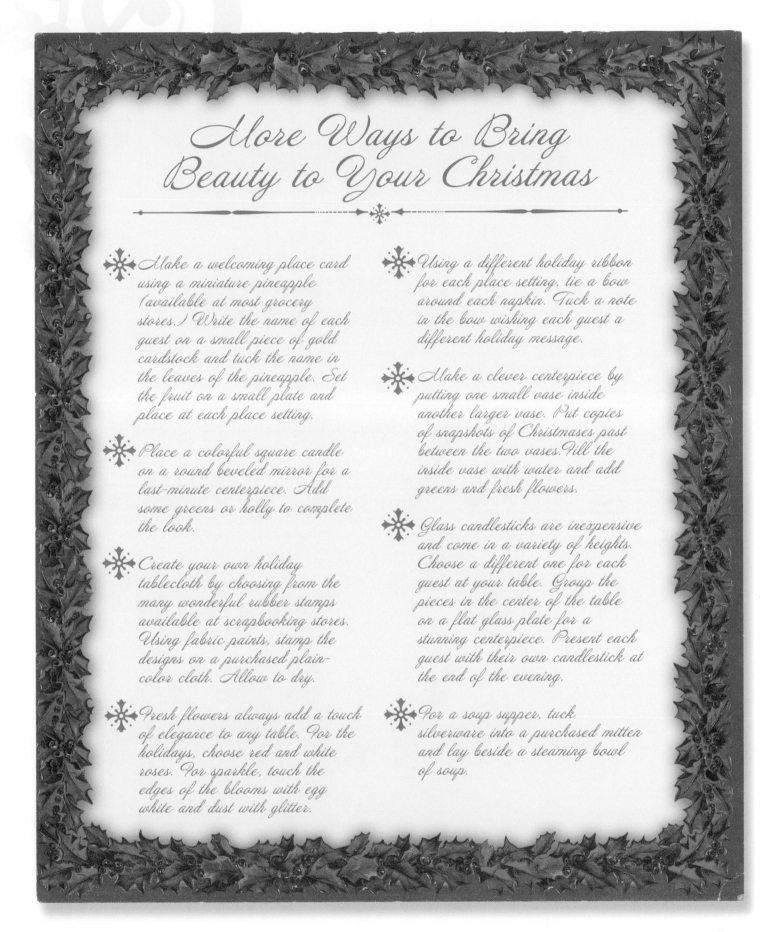

More Ways to Bring Beauty to Your Christmas

❄ Make a welcoming place card using a miniature pineapple (available at most grocery stores.) Write the name of each guest on a small piece of gold cardstock and tuck the name in the leaves of the pineapple. Set the fruit on a small plate and place at each place setting.

❄ Place a colorful square candle on a round beveled mirror for a last-minute centerpiece. Add some greens or holly to complete the look.

❄ Create your own holiday tablecloth by choosing from the many wonderful rubber stamps available at scrapbooking stores. Using fabric paints, stamp the designs on a purchased plain-color cloth. Allow to dry.

❄ Fresh flowers always add a touch of elegance to any table. For the holidays, choose red and white roses. For sparkle, touch the edges of the blooms with egg white and dust with glitter.

❄ Using a different holiday ribbon for each place setting, tie a bow around each napkin. Tuck a note in the bow wishing each guest a different holiday message.

❄ Make a clever centerpiece by putting one small vase inside another larger vase. Put copies of snapshots of Christmases past between the two vases. Fill the inside vase with water and add greens and fresh flowers.

❄ Glass candlesticks are inexpensive and come in a variety of heights. Choose a different one for each guest at your table. Group the pieces in the center of the table on a flat glass plate for a stunning centerpiece. Present each guest with their own candlestick at the end of the evening.

❄ For a soup supper, tuck silverware into a purchased mitten and lay beside a steaming bowl of soup.

simmered

Beautifully

arranged

presented

decorated

sliced

frosted

sugared

baked

Christmas Cookies and Wintertime Favorites

The kitchen is the place they gather when Christmas is near. This year, fill your kitchen with all kinds of homemade goodies. Artful cookies, smooth and rich candies, red-berry pies, steaming soups, simple appetizers, clever cut-up cakes, and rich cheesy crackers are just a few of the oh-so-delicious recipes you'll find in this holiday-inspired chapter.

GINGERBREAD STENCIL COOKIES

The dark richness of gingerbread combines with delicate pastel sugars to make a delightful Christmas treat.

Refer to stencil patterns on *page 110*.

What you need:

- Tracing paper
- Stencil paper or lightweight cardboard
- Crafts knife

• • •

- 5½ cups flour
- 2 teaspoons ground ginger
- 2 teaspoons ground cinnamon
- ½ teaspoon ground cloves
- ¾ teaspoon baking soda
- ¼ teaspoon baking powder
- 1 cup butter, softened
- 1 cup packed dark brown sugar
- 1 cup light molasses
- 2 eggs
- Vanilla Powdered Sugar Icing (recipe, page 109)
- Fine, colored decorating sugars (available at fine cook's ware stores or mail order, see sources, page 159)

What you do:

Refer to stencil patterns on *page 110*. Trace and transfer to stencil paper or cardboard. Cut around outside shape; cut out colored areas with crafts knife. Set aside.

In a large bowl stir together flour, ginger, cinnamon, cloves, baking soda, and baking powder.

In another bowl beat butter with an electric mixer. Beat in brown sugar until fluffy. Beat in molasses and eggs until well combined. Gradually beat in flour mixture. Use a wooden spoon if dough is too thick for mixer. Divide dough in half. Wrap dough in plastic wrap and

POINSETTIA COOKIES

Roll out a favorite cookie dough and cut with a 4-inch circle cutter. Bake as directed; cool. Following the instructions as for gingerbread cookies, decorate using the poinsettia stencil pattern on page 110.

chill several hours or until easy to handle. On a lightly floured surface roll out one portion of dough to ¼-inch thickness. Cut out cookies with cookie cutters. Place 1 inch apart on lightly greased cookie sheet. Bake in a 375° oven for 8 to 10 minutes or until cookies are firm in center. Cool for 2 to 3 minutes on cookie sheet. Remove cookies to a wire rack to cool. Repeat with remaining dough. Makes 4 to 5 dozen cookies.

Decorate about one dozen cookies at a time. With a spatula spread some icing on top of cookies, spreading to, but not over, the cookie edges. Let icing dry 5 to 10 minutes or until surface is just dry to the touch. Place a cookie stencil carefully on top of just dry icing. Sprinkle some colored sugar over stencil. Carefully lift stencil and shake off excess sugar. Repeat stenciling steps with iced cookies before icing another batch of

cookies. Allow sugared cookies to dry several hours before handling. *Note:* Silver or colored dragees are for decoration only. Always remove before eating.

Vanilla Powdered Sugar Icing: In a medium bowl, stir together 2 cups sifted powdered sugar, 1 tablespoon vanilla, and enough milk (1 to 3 tablespoons) to make spreading consistency. Add the milk gradually until desired consistency is reached.

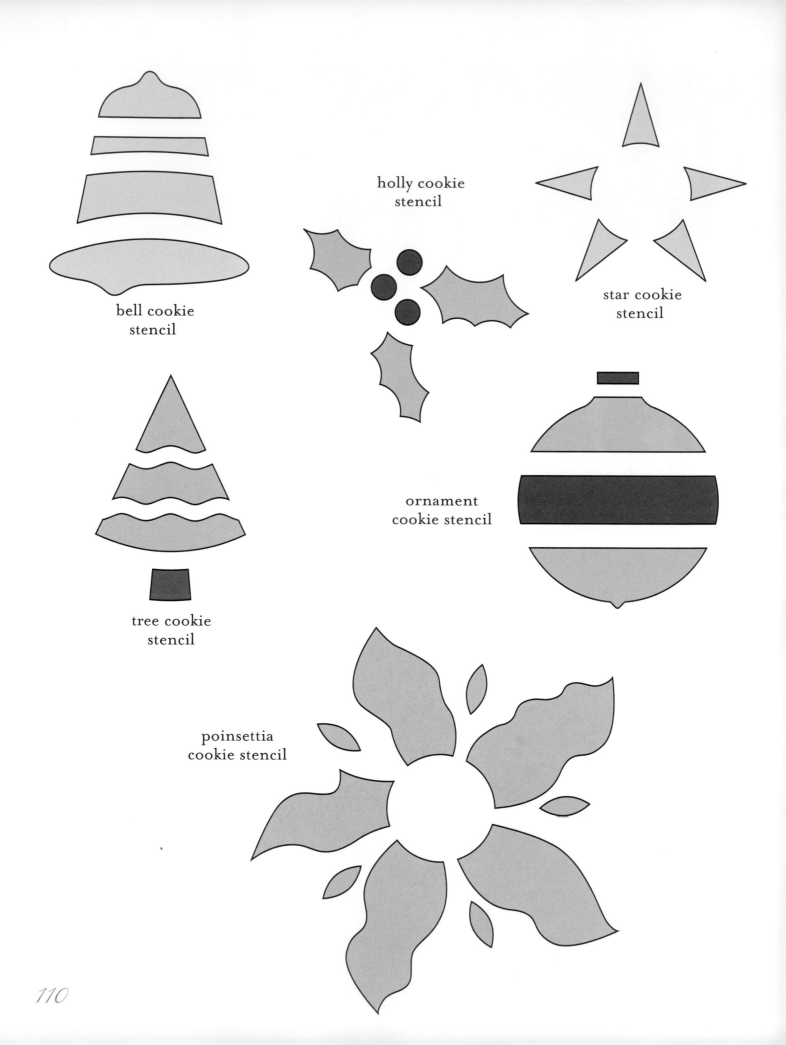

bell cookie
stencil

holly cookie
stencil

star cookie
stencil

tree cookie
stencil

ornament
cookie stencil

poinsettia
cookie stencil

HOLIDAY ICEBOX COOKIES

This recipe is a family favorite, enjoyed years ago at holiday time when the "icebox" was a real luxury.

What you do:

Cut up fruits and nuts and place in small bowl. Set aside. In a large bowl, beat butter, granulated sugar, brown sugar, vanilla, and egg. In another bowl, mix flour, soda, and salt. Add fruit and nuts to the flour mixture. Add to the butter and sugar mixture and mix well.

Shape into 2 logs about 2 inches in diameter. Wrap in plastic wrap and foil. Refrigerate dough logs overnight.

When ready to bake, cut into slices about ½ inch thick. Place on greased cookie sheet and bake in a 350° oven for 12 minutes or until lightly brown. Makes about 2 dozen cookies.

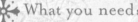

What you need:

- 2 cups fruit (candied pineapple, golden raisins, candied cherries, dates, dried apricots)
- 2 cups nuts (pecans, walnuts, brazil nuts)
- 1 cup plus 2 tablespoons butter
- ⅓ cup granulated sugar
- ⅓ cup packed brown sugar
- 1 teaspoon vanilla
- 1 egg
- 1⅔ cups flour
- ¾ teaspoon baking soda
- ½ teaspoon salt

Christmas red and green are appropriate colors for the ingredients in these holiday goodie bars.

❋ What you need:

Bottom layer:
- ⅓ cup butter, softened
- ½ cup granulated sugar
- 1 egg
- 1 teaspoon vanilla
- 1¼ cups flour

Top layer:
- ⅓ cup butter, melted
- ⅓ cup packed brown sugar
- ⅓ cup pistachio nuts, chopped
- ⅓ cup flaked coconut
- 12 maraschino cherries, drained and cut up
- 3 tablespoons water

❋ What you do:

For bottom layer, in a small bowl, beat butter and sugar. Add egg, vanilla, and flour. Mix well. Pat into a 9x13-inch baking pan. Set aside. For the top layer, in another small bowl, beat butter and sugar. Add pistachio nuts, coconut, maraschino cherries, and water. Spread over bottom layer. Press lightly. Bake in a 350° oven for 20-25 minutes. Drizzle with Vanilla Powdered Sugar Icing, *page 109*, if desired. Cut into squares while warm. Makes 36 small bars.

PEANUT BUTTER BEAUTIES

Favorite peanut butter cookies are dressed up for the holidays with sugar and pecans or a candy motif.

 What you do:

In a large bowl, beat together the butter, brown sugar, and granulated sugar. Add eggs, peanut butter, and vanilla. In another bowl, mix together flour and baking soda. Combine with the creamed mixture and mix together until well combined. Dough should be stiff. Roll in balls about the size of a walnut and dip in sugar if desired. Add pecan half or leave plain for candy decoration. Bake in a 350° oven for 8 minutes. Place chocolate candy in center of plain cookies. Bake 2½ minutes more. Remove from oven and allow to cool on wire rack. Makes 5 dozen cookies.

What you need:
- 1 cup butter
- 1 cup packed brown sugar
- 1 cup granulated sugar
- 2 eggs
- 1 cup peanut butter
- 1 teaspoon vanilla
- 3 cups flour
- 2 teaspoons baking soda
- Pecan halves
- Purchased holiday chocolate candies

Turn simple squares of cake into sweet presents that anticipate delicate white-cake flavor.

❄ **What you need:**

- **One two-layer yellow cake mix**
- **Petits Fours Icing (recipe, page 115)**
- **Purchased rolled fondant**
- **Paste food coloring**
- **About 1 cup Decorator Frosting (recipe, page 115)**

❄ **What you do:**

Prepare cake mix as directed on package except reduce water by ¼ cup. Grease a 9-inch square cake pan. Line bottom of pan with waxed paper. Fill pan ⅔ full with batter. (Use remaining batter to make cupcakes.) Bake in a 350° oven for 35 to 40 minutes or until a toothpick inserted comes out clean. Cool in pan for 10 minutes. Invert cake onto a waxed paper-lined wire rack. Remove waxed paper that lined cake pan. Cool cake completely. Cut cake into 9 square pieces. Let cake pieces dry about 1 hour. Meanwhile, prepare Petits Fours Icing. Insert a long-handled fork into side of one cake piece. Holding cake over the saucepan of icing, spoon icing over cake to cover the sides and top. Place frosted cake on a wire rack. Repeat with remaining cake pieces. If desired, add a second coat of icing. If icing becomes too thick, beat in a few drops of hot water.

To make rolled fondant bows, knead tiny amounts of paste food coloring into small portions of fondant. Keep fondant covered when not using. On a smooth surface that has been lightly dusted with powdered sugar, roll

So Easy

❄ *To make the look-alike centerpiece, wrap a square box with striped paper. Set the box in the center of the table and surround with greens and ornaments.*

fondant pieces into small logs. Use a rolling pin to flatten the logs to about ⅛-inch thickness. Using a ruler as a guide, cut fondant into narrow strips with a table knife. Decorate the frosted cake pieces with the strips. If necessary, lightly brush strips of fondant with water to help them stick to icing. For bows, bend strips into tiny loops. Gently press them on top of the cakes. For added decorations, divide the 1 cup of Decorator Frosting into 4 portions. Tint each with paste

food coloring. Place in decorating bags fitted with couplers and tips. Pipe dots and stripes onto cakes. Cakes can be stored for 1 or 2 days in a loosely covered cake container.

Petits Fours Icing

In a medium saucepan combine 3 cups granulated sugar, 1½ cups hot water, and ¼ teaspoon cream of tartar. Bring to boiling, stirring constantly, until the sugar dissolves (5 to 7 minutes). Beat in 4 to 5 cups sifted

powdered sugar and 2 teaspoons clear vanilla until smooth.

Decorator Frosting

In a large mixing bowl beat 1 cup shortening, 2 teaspoons clear vanilla, and ½ teaspoon almond extract. Gradually beat in 2 cups sifted powdered sugar. Beat in 2 tablespoons milk. Gradually beat in 2 cups additional powdered sugar and enough milk (2 to 3 tablespoons) to make a frosting that is creamy and holds a stiff peak. Makes about 3 cups.

LACE COOKIES

These delicate cookies bake up almost like magic.

What you do:

In a large bowl, beat the butter and sugar. Add remaining ingredients and mix well. Roll ¹/₂ teaspoon of batter into a ball. Place on parchment lined cookie sheet. Flatten slightly with fork. Place two inches apart.

Bake for 7-8 minutes in 350° oven. Cool 1 minute before removing from sheet. Makes 3 dozen cookies.

Family Affair

These cookies call for just a few simple ingredients and bake in such an unexpected way that the kids will love to be in on the magic. Serve with a favorite ice cream for a special Christmas treat.

SUGARY WINDOW COOKIES
Almost as beautiful as a stained glass window, these cookies are remarkably easy to make.

 What you do:

Divide sugar cookie dough in half. Set one half aside. Divide the other half into 6 portions. Tint each portion with a different food coloring. Roll each tinted portion into a long ½x6-inch shape. Roll out the uncolored portion of the cookie dough into a rectangle about 4x6-inches and about ¼-inch thick. Stack the colored dough logs inside the center of the rectangle; wrap the uncolored portion around the colored logs and seal. Wrap with plastic wrap; chill for one hour.

Remove wrap and slice cookies ½-inch thick. Sprinkle with coarse sugar. Bake according to package instructions. Cool. Makes about 24 cookies.

What you need:
- Purchased sugar cookie dough (1 lb. 2 oz. package)
- Food coloring
- Coarse granulated sugar

❄ **What you need:**

- **1 cup granulated sugar**
- **⅓ cup flour**
- **½ teaspoon ground cinnamon**
- **2 teaspoons finely shredded orange peel**
- **1½ packages (12 oz. each) frozen mixed berries (raspberries, strawberries, blueberries, blackberries)**
- **15 oz. package refrigerated piecrust dough**
- **Milk**
- **1 egg**
- **1 tablespoon water**
- **Green and red liquid food coloring**
- **Granulated sugar**

HOLIDAY BERRY PIE

Just a little pie crust cut in the shape of holly makes this pie special for Christmas dinner.

❄ What you do:

In a large bowl combine sugar, flour, cinnamon, and orange peel. Stir in frozen berries. Let stand 45 minutes to thaw. On a lightly floured surface, roll out 2 pie crust circles to 13 inches.

Line a deep dish 9-inch pie plate with one circle of dough. Spoon berry mixture into piecrust. Brush edge of crust with milk. Place top crust on pie; trim edge of crust to 1 inch beyond edge of pie plate. Save scraps. Turn edges of crust under; pinch to seal. Roll out scraps of dough on floured surface. Referring to pattern, *below*, cut out holly leaf shapes berries. In small bowl, beat 1 egg and 1 tablespoon water. Brush top of pie with egg mixture. Arrange leaves and berries on pie crust. Divide remaining egg mixture in half. Tint 1 portion green and other portion red. Paint leaves with green mixture and berries with red mixture. Pierce top crust four to five times with fork. Sprinkle top of pie with sugar.

Cover top of pie with foil. Bake in a 375° oven for 50 minutes. Remove foil. Bake an additional 25 to 30 minutes or until filling is bubbly and piecrust is golden. Cool on a wire rack. Serves 8.

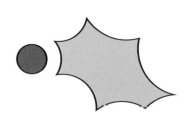

holly leaf pattern

RASPBERRY RIBBON COOKIES

Just like the ribbon on those carefully wrapped gifts, these cookies make that cookie tray even prettier.

 What you do:

In a large bowl, beat together the butter, cream cheese, milk, and sugar. Add beaten egg yolk. Sift together flour and baking powder. Add to butter mixture and beat well. Wrap in plastic wrap and chill for 4 hours.

Divide dough into 8 equal portions. Roll each piece into a rope about 10 inches long and 1 inch in diameter. Place ropes 2 inches apart on ungreased cookie sheets. Using the blunt edge of a table knife, press ⅛-inch-deep grooves into dough. Bake in 350° oven for 10 minutes. Remove cookies from oven. Fill a pastry bag with ⅓ cup seedless jam. With a ¼-inch tip, pipe jam into groove. Return cookies to oven for 5 more minutes.

In a small bowl, stir together 1 tablespoon lemon juice and ½ cup powdered sugar. Stir until glaze drops easily from spoon. Drizzle across hot cookies.

While still warm, use a sharp knife to cut the cookies diagonally into 2-inch strips. Cool on a wire rack. Makes 4–5 dozen cookies.

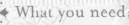 What you need:
- 1 cup butter, softened
- 8 oz. package cream cheese
- 1 tablespoon milk
- 1 tablespoon granulated sugar
- 1 egg yolk, beaten
- 2 cups flour
- ½ teaspoon baking powder
- ½ cup sifted powdered sugar
- 1 tablespoon lemon juice
- 12 oz. jar seedless raspberry jam

To Give

❄ *Stack these homestyle cookies in an antique brown crock and wrap with brown paper and a rustic-patterned ribbon for a perfect gift from the kitchen.*

❄ What you need:
- **I cup shortening**
- **I cup granulated sugar**
- **I cup packed brown sugar**
- **3 eggs**
- **4 cups flour**
- **¼ teaspoon salt**
- **I teaspoon baking soda**
- **I teaspoon vanilla**
- **I cup chopped nut meats**
- **I jar prepared mincemeat (27 oz.)**

OLD FASHIONED MINCEMEAT COOKIES
This delicious combination of flavors brings back memories of Christmases past.

❄ What you do:

In a large bowl, mix shortening, granulated sugar, brown sugar, and eggs. Add the flour, salt, baking soda, and vanilla. Mix until well combined. Divide dough into 2 parts. Roll dough to ¼ inch on a floured surface. Use a spatula to spread the dough with mincemeat. Sprinkle with ½ cup nuts. Roll up dough and seal edges. Wrap in plastic wrap. Repeat using remaining dough. Chill the cookie rolls for at least 4 hours or overnight.

When ready to bake, slice dough to ¼ inch thick. Bake on a greased cookie sheet in a 350° oven for 10-15 minutes. Makes about 5 dozen cookies.

CHRISTMAS MORNING COFFEE CAKE

So moist and flavorful, this coffee cake will bring smiles on Christmas morning.

What you do:

Grease and flour a 9x13-inch baking pan. Set aside. In a large bowl, mix together the flour, brown sugar, granulated sugar, cinnamon, nutmeg, and salt. Add the oil. Mix until moist.

Measure out 1 cup of the crumb mixture and set aside for the coffee cake topping. Stir together the egg, buttermilk, and soda. Make a well in the middle of the flour mixture and add the buttermilk mixture. Mix well. Spread in the prepared pan.

Sprinkle the 1 cup crumbs on top of the coffee cake. Add crushed candies if desired. Bake in a 350° oven for 45 minutes. Serve warm. Serves 16.

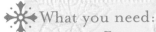 What you need:

- 3 cups flour
- 1 cup packed brown sugar
- 1 cup granulated sugar
- 1 teaspoon cinnamon
- 1 teaspoon ground nutmeg
- 1 teaspoon salt
- 1 cup cooking oil
- 1 egg
- 1 cup buttermilk
- 1 teaspoon baking soda
- Crushed candy canes

GERMAN GOOD LUCK COOKIES

These beautiful cookies are decorated in the German tradition of the 12 symbols of a happy home.

❄ **What you need:**
- 3 cups flour
- I teaspoon baking powder
- ¼ teaspoon salt
- I cup butter, softened
- I cup granulated sugar
- I egg
- 2 teaspoons vanilla
- 3 tablespoons milk
- Decorator Frosting (page 115)
- Decorating bags, couplers and tips (star, round, rose)
- Paste food coloring (red, kelly green, gray, golden yellow, brown, purple)
- Fine sugar
- Cookie cutter (see sources, page 159)

❄ **What you do:**

In a large bowl stir together flour, baking powder, and salt. In another bowl beat butter with an electric mixer. Beat in sugar until fluffy. Beat in egg until well combined. Mix in vanilla and milk. Gradually beat in flour mixture. Divide dough into 2 portions. Wrap in plastic wrap and chill several hours.

Roll out chilled dough on a lightly floured surface to about ¼-inch thickness. Cut out shapes

with cookie cutters. Place cookies 1 inch apart on lightly greased cookie sheet. Bake in a 375° oven for 6 to 8 minutes or until edges just begin to brown. Let cool on cookie sheet for 2 minutes. Cool on wire rack. Makes about 3 to 4 dozen cookies.

Divide frosting for tinting. Add a small amount of food coloring to make colors shown. Leave about ⅓ of the frosting white. Place colored and white frostings in decorating bags fitted with couplers. Use desired tips to decorate the cookies as shown. If desired, sprinkle frosted cookies with fine sanding sugar.

12 Symbols of a Happy Home

Heart . . . . . .love
Rabbit . . . . .hope
Flowers . . . . . .beauty
Bird . . . . . .joy
Rose . . . . . .affection
House . . . . . .protection
Fruit Basket . .generosity
Pinecone . . . .fruitfulness
Fish . . . . . . .blessings
Teapot . . . . .hospitality
Santa . . . . .goodwill
Angel . . . . . .guidance

123

Pretty Cut-Up Cakes

Whether you prefer a Beautiful Star, a clever Christmas Tree, or a Golden Bell, each of these cut-up cakes can measure up to just what you have in mind for the holidays. The star is trimmed in white coconut, the Christmas tree has pretty scallops, and the bell is decorated with rolled fondant.

You'll surprise your family and friends with your cake-decorating talent when you present one of these glorious holiday cakes.

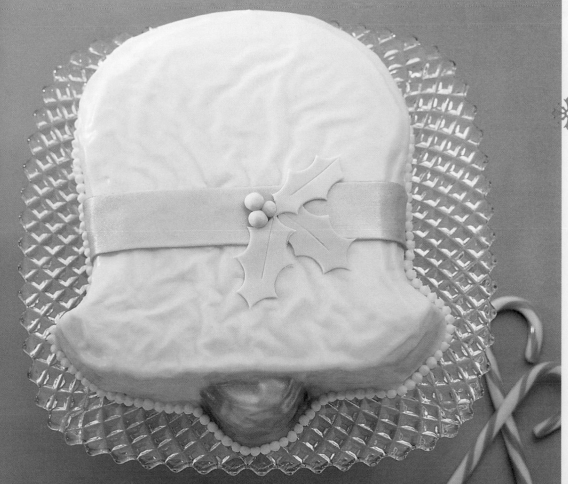

So Easy

❄ Even though these cakes look elegant, they are surprisingly easy to make. Each cake is made from a purchased mix and baked in rectangular, round, or square pans. The trick to making the cakes is how the cake is cut up and then put back together. Frosting the cake disguises the magical cutting you do.

continued on page 126

125

BEAUTIFUL STAR CAKE

Two round cakes are cleverly cut to create this beautiful symbol of Christmas.

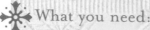
What you need:
- Tracing paper
- Two baked 8-inch round cake layers
- Decorator Frosting (recipe, page 115)
- 1 cup flaked coconut
- Gold dragees

What you do:

Enlarge star cake pattern, *opposite*, onto tracing paper; cut out. Place pattern on top of each cake layer and trim edges. Remove pattern and cut on dotted lines. Place on one of trimmed layers. Cut cake into 5 equal cake wedges. On cake plate arrange the 5-sided cake layer in center. Arrange the 5 wedges of cake around the center cake layer forming a large star shape. Frost the top and sides of cake with Decorator Frosting. Place gold dragees in a garland design. Sprinkle cake with coconut. Makes 10 servings. *Note:* Dragees are for decoration only. Always remove before eating.

CHRISTMAS TREE CAKE

Your family and friends won't believe that you trimmed this tree with frosting all by yourself!

What you need:
- Tracing paper
- One baked 9x13x2-inch cake
- One recipe Petits Fours Icing (recipe, page 115)
- Green and yellow liquid food coloring
- ½ cup Decorator Frosting (page 115)
- Decorating bag fitted with very small round tip

What you do:

Draw a 9x13-inch rectangle onto tracing paper and following the diagram, *opposite*, mark the cut out lines on the drawing. Cut out the pattern pieces and reassemble them on top of the 9x13-inch cake. With a serrated knife, cut cake into pattern-size pieces. There will be 2 small triangles, 2 large triangles, and 1 rectangle. Arrange the cake pieces on a large serving tray to resemble a Christmas tree. Alternately tilt the triangles for a whimsical look. Cut away the peaks of the bottom 3 triangles to allow cakes to fit together. Tuck strips of waxed paper under edges of cake to catch excess icing. To prepare the Petits Fours Icing, immediately tint the icing using a few drops of green and yellow food coloring. Carefully spoon over tops and edges of cake pieces until all of cake is covered. Remove the waxed paper strips and excess icing. Tint Decorator Frosting with a drop of yellow food coloring to make frosting a creamy pale yellow color. Place in a decorating bag fitted with a very small round tip. Pipe a dotted garland on top of cake. Serves 10 to 12.

GOLDEN BELL CAKE

This holiday bell cake is so easy to make. Just sculpt the cake and frost with golden frosting.

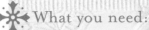

What you need:
- **Tracing paper**
- **One 9-inch round cake layer**
- **½ of Petits Fours Icing (page 115)**
- **½ cup purchased rolled fondant**
- **Yellow and green paste food coloring**
- **Gold luster dust, optional (see sources, page 159)**

What you do: Enlarge and trace the bell pattern, *below.* Place on cake layer and trim with a serrated knife. Remove pattern and sculpt with serrated knife by trimming top edges of cake so bell has a rounded top edge. Trim the ball (clapper) into a rounded shape. Place cake on serving plate. Tuck waxed paper under edges of cake to catch excess icing.

Prepare Petits Fours Icing. Immediately tint icing yellow. Carefully spoon icing over top and sides of cake until cake is covered. Let icing dry for at least 2 hours. Meanwhile tint about ¾ of the fondant with a toothpick

dipped in yellow paste food coloring. Divide remaining fondant in half. Tint one portion green and one portion dark yellow. Keep all fondant covered with plastic wrap when not using. On a surface dusted with powdered sugar, roll the yellow fondant into an 8-inch log. Use a rolling pin to flatten the log to about ¹/₁₆-inch thickness. Cut into a ¾-inch strip. Lay strip across middle of bell. Trim ends of strip even with bottom of cake. Roll out green fondant to ¹/₁₆-inch thickness. Use a sharp knife to cut out 1-inch leaf shapes. Place three leaves on cake top, overlapping ribbon. Roll dark yellow fondant into several ball shapes and

attach to leaves. If necessary, brush shapes lightly with water to help them stick. If desired, use a clean dry artist's brush to apply gold luster dust to the yellow ribbon and clapper of bell. Serves 6.

star cake

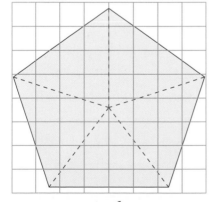

I square=1 inch
enlarge 400%

tree cake

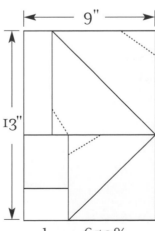

9"

13"

enlarge 650%

bell cake

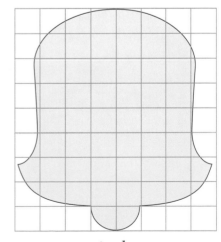

I square=1 inch
enlarge 400%

FAIRYLAND COOKIES

Magic fills the air with these sweet cookies. To decorate a tree with these lovely creatures, see pages 34-35.

What you need:

- 3 cups flour
- 1 teaspoon baking powder
- ¼ teaspoon salt
- 1 cup butter, softened
- 1 cup granulated sugar
- 1 egg
- 2 teaspoons vanilla
- 3 tablespoons milk
- Meringue Icing (recipe, page 129)
- 1 decorating bag
- Paste food coloring (peach, pink, lavender, leaf green, blue, golden yellow)
- Cookie cutters, (see sources, page 159)

What you do:

In a large bowl stir together flour, baking powder, and salt. In another bowl beat butter with an electric mixer. Beat in sugar until well combined and fluffy. Beat in egg until well combined. Beat in vanilla and milk. Gradually beat in flour mixture, using a spoon if too thick for mixer. Divide dough into 2 portions. Wrap in plastic wrap and chill several hours or until easy to handle.

Roll out chilled dough on a lightly floured surface to about ¼ to ⅛ inch thick. Cut out shapes with cookie cutters. Place cutouts 1 inch apart on lightly greased cookie sheet. Use the end of a straw to make small holes at the top of cookies for hanging. Bake in a 375° oven for 8 to 10 minutes or until edges just begin to brown. Cool on cookie sheet for 2 minutes. Remove to a wire rack to cool completely. Makes 3 to 4 dozen cookies.

Place about ⅓ cup white Meringue Icing in a decorating bag. Twist bag shut and seal with a twist tie. Do not snip tip of bag

To Give

For a special gift, place one of these beautiful winged wonders in a parchment envelope. Punch two holes in the top of the envelope and add a satin ribbon. Write the name on the envelope with a blue metallic marker.

128

until ready to use. Divide remaining Meringue Icing among small bowls. Keep icing covered when not using. Tint icing desired colors with a small amount of paste food coloring. Add a few drops of water to icing colors in bowls until each is flowing consistency. Using a small, clean artist's brush, paint the thinned icing onto cookies. Snip a tiny opening at end of bag. Pipe white icing outlines and details onto cookies. Let dry completely (about 2 hours) before threading with a ribbon and hanging on tree.

Meringue Icing:
In a medium bowl beat together 3 tablespoons meringue powder, $\frac{1}{2}$ teaspoon cream of tartar, 1 teaspoon clear vanilla, and $\frac{1}{2}$ cup warm water with an electric mixer. Beat in $4\frac{1}{2}$ cups sifted powdered sugar on low speed until combined. Beat on high speed for about 5 minutes or until thickened. Makes about 3 cups.

TWELVE DAYS OF CHRISTMAS COOKIES

You'll welcome the last few days before Christmas with such festive ideas as these candy-dipped cookies.

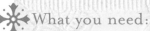

What you need:

- 1 package vanilla cream-filled sandwich cookies (about 4 dozen)
- 24 oz. vanilla-flavored candy coating
- 1 tablespoon shortening
- Chocolate, green, yellow, and red candy coating discs (about ½ cup each)
- 4 decorating bags

What you do:

In a large microwave-safe bowl place vanilla candy coating and shortening. Microwave on high for 1 minute. Stir. Continue to microwave and stir until melted. With a fork, dip cookies one at a time into melted mixture. Shake off excess candy coating. Place on a wire rack to set up.

Place chocolate, green, yellow, and red candy coating in small microwave-safe bowls or glass custard cups. Melt in microwave for about 1 minute or until smooth when stirred. Place melted coatings in decorator bags. Twist the ends to close the bags. Snip a small opening at tip of each bag. Pipe designs as shown on coated cookies and referring to patterns, *opposite*. If coating in bag becomes cooled and hardened, place the bag in the microwave and heat for about 30 seconds.

FRUIT FLAVORED DIVINITY

The secret to these beautiful Christmas-colored candies is just a touch of colored gelatin.

What you do:

In a heavy saucepan, stir together the sugar, corn syrup, hot water, salt, and gelatin. Bring the mixture to boiling. Boil until the mixture reaches a temperature of 250° F on a candy thermometer, stirring occasionally.

Beat the egg whites until stiff. Slowly pour the hot syrup into the egg whites, beating on high until mixture is stiff and loses its gloss. Add vanilla. Add nuts if desired. Drop by rounded teaspoonfuls onto waxed paper. Makes about 35 pieces.

Family Affair

Any color or flavor of gelatin can be added to the candy. Have the children pick their favorite flavors and let them add the pretty colored granules to the candy. It is almost like magic to watch the divinity turn a pretty pastel color.

132

COCONUT CANDIES
They'll be coming back for more when they taste these lovely coconut favorites.

❄ What you do for the Coconut Fudge:

In a large saucepan, combine all ingredients except pecans and coconut. Cook, stirring until mixture reaches 235° F on candy thermometer. Cool for 20 minutes. Add vanilla and beat until creamy. Stir in pecans and coconut. Pour into buttered 8x8-inch pan. Cool; cut into squares. Makes 36 pieces.

❄ What you do for the Coconut Dates:

Remove pits from the dates. Fill with strawberry cream cheese. Stuff pecan into the cream cheese. Dip the stuffed date into Fluffy Icing. Place onto parchment paper. Top with coconut. Serve immediately. Makes 12 candies.

Fluffy Icing:

1 cup granulated sugar
1 tablespoon white corn syrup
1/3 cup water
2 egg whites
1/4 teaspoon cream of tartar
1 teaspoon vanilla
10 small marshmallows

In a heavy saucepan, mix the sugar, corn syrup, and water. Boil until the mixture reaches 250° F on a candy thermometer. Set aside. With a mixer, beat the egg whites and cream of tartar on high speed for 1 minute. Slowly pour hot syrup mixture into the beaten egg whites while continuing to beat on high speed. Beat for 5 minutes. Add the vanilla and marshmallows and beat 1 more minute.

❄ What you need for the White Coconut Fudge:

- 2 cups granulated sugar
- 1/3 cup white corn syrup
- 1/2 cup drained, crushed pineapple
- 1/2 cup light cream
- 1 tablespoon butter
- 1 teaspoon vanilla
- 1/2 cup chopped pecans
- 1/2 cup flaked coconut

❄ What you need for the Coconut Dates:

- 12 large dates
- 12 pecan halves
- 1/2 cup strawberry cream cheese
- Fluffy Icing, left
- 1/2 cup flaked coconut

Coconut Fudge

Coconut Dates

So Easy

❄ *Even if you only have a little time before the party begins, you can make these clever wraps. Try adding other things you have on hand such as mushrooms, pimentos, or sweet peppers.*

HOLIDAY WRAPS

Red and green tortillas make these wraps all dressed up for the holidays.

❄ **What you need:**
- **Tortillas(we used red and green tortillas)**
- **6 oz. package cream cheese**
- **8 oz. package thinly sliced ham**
- **8 oz. bag shredded co-jack cheese**
- **Fresh chives, washed and chopped**
- **Pitted olives**

❄ **What you do:**

Lay the tortilla on a flat surface. Using a knife or spatula, spread the tortilla evenly with the cream cheese. Use about 3 tablespoons of cream cheese on each tortilla. Layer slices of ham, shredded cheese, chives, and sliced olives on top of the cream cheese. Roll up tightly. Wrap in plastic wrap or foil and seal. Chill for at least 1 hour.

Remove plastic or foil and slice the tortilla wrap into 2 inch pieces to serve. Each tortilla makes about 5 pieces.

TOMATO BASIL SOUP

Perfect for a soup supper after Christmas caroling, this tangy soup will become a yearly tradition.

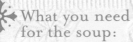 **What you do for the soup:**

In a large heavy saucepan, melt the butter. Stir in the flour until blended. Add the chicken broth. Simmer until thick. Add the vegetable juice, diced tomatoes, basil, salt, and pepper. Simmer until ready to eat. Garnish with sour cream. Serves 6.

To make the monogram letter, place cold sour cream into a decorator bag. Pipe the monogram on the soup just before serving.

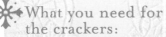 **What you do for the crackers:**

In a small bowl, beat the butter and the flour. Add the shredded cheese and rice cereal. Mix well. Form into 1-inch balls.

Place the balls on a greased cookie sheet. Flatten the balls with a damp fork. Bake in a 325° oven for about 20 minutes.

Remove from oven and cool on wire rack. Makes about 3 dozen crackers.

❄ **What you need for the soup:**
- 2 tablespoons butter
- 2 tablespoons flour
- 14 oz. can chicken broth
- 2 cups vegetable juice, such as V8
- 1 large can (1 lb. 4 oz.) diced tomatoes
- 2 tablespoons snipped fresh basil or 1 teaspoon dried basil, crushed
- Salt and pepper to taste
- Sour cream

❄ **What you need for the crackers:**
- 1 cup butter
- 2 cups flour
- 2 cups shredded cheddar cheese
- 2 cups crisp rice cereal

HEARTY RED POTATO SOUP

Choose pretty red potatoes for this creamy soup to make a colorful presentation.

❄ **What you need:**

- **2 cups cooked red-skin potatoes**
- **I tablespoon butter**
- **¼ cup chopped red pepper**
- **¼ cup chopped green pepper**
- **¼ cup chopped celery**
- **¼ cup chopped onion**
- **I tablespoon flour**
- **½ cup milk**
- **I cup chicken broth**
- **¾ cup frozen or fresh peas**
- **I cup milk**
- **I cup light cream**
- **Salt and pepper to taste**

❄ What you do:

Cook potatoes in boiling water with skins on. Drain and set aside. In a heavy saucepan, melt the butter. Sauté red pepper, green pepper, celery, and onion. Combine flour with the ½ cup milk. Add to the vegetables in the saucepan. Cook until thickened. Add chicken broth and peas and bring to a boil. Boil I minute. Add the I cup milk and cream. Heat but do not boil. Slice cooked potatoes and add to mixture. Add salt and pepper, and serve immediately. Serves 8.

More Ways to Bring Beauty to Your Christmas

When presenting your holiday dishes this year, don't forget the garnishes. Use thin slices of lemon, sprigs of fresh mint, pretty carrot curls, or a strip of twisted orange rind to garnish the lovely platters and plates that hold your special recipes.

Go to the candy shop and choose your favorite chocolate-dipped candies. During the holiday season, there are wonderful shapes and flavors. Add these little treats to your homemade cookie tray for added sweetness.

Make a quick Christmas punch by combining cranberry juice with lemon-lime soda. Pour in a punch bowl and float slices of oranges cut into star shapes.

Make your Christmas cookies even prettier by adding a drop of red food coloring to the sugar cookie dough. The pastel pink color will add an unexpected holiday touch.

Combine fresh fruits for a stunning centerpiece. Start by setting a pineapple in the center of a large glass plate. Surround it with pomegranates, star fruit, limes, kumquats, and tangerines. Sprinkle fresh cranberries on top of the arrangement.

Using large cookie cutters, cut bread into holiday shapes before making French toast for Christmas morning breakfast. Serve raspberry syrup and red jellies and jams with this fun-shaped French toast to make the breakfast complete.

Give your special homemade Christmas cookies in clever wraps. Try stacking them in a canning jar decorated with stickers, placing them in a small gift bag decorated with rubber stamping, or tying them up in cellophane with a holiday ribbon.

Crush peppermint candy canes to have on hand to sprinkle on cakes, cookies, and ice cream.

folded

Beautifully

cropped

stamped

cut

arranged

glittered

embellished

colored

Paper Greetings and Handmade Memories

Whether you are creating handmade
greeting cards or scrapbooking lovely paper
pages, your friends and family will
appreciate your talents. Have fun making
these paper memories using glitter, stickers,
fibers, stamps, and other embellishments
that make your work one-of-a-kind.

THREE KITTENS CARD

Send a fairy tale greeting this year to wish your friends and family a Merry Christmas and a happily ever after.

❄ What you do:

Color copy or scan the art, *below*. Using small scissors or a crafts knife, cut out. Set aside. Measure ¼-inch from the edge of the long side of the larger piece of the sage green cardstock. Mark with a pencil and score along that line. Fold along the scored line. Glue the smaller piece of sage green cardstock to the folded edge making a folded card. On the card front, center the soft green cardstock ¼-inch from the bottom. Use the glue stick to glue in place. At the top of the card, place the letter stickers in two

rows spelling "Fairy Tale Christmas". Glue the kitty cutout on top of the soft green square and overlapping some of the heading letters. See the photo, *above*, for placement of the kitty cutout. Use the white crafts glue to make a fine line around the soft green cardstock. Dust with fine gold glitter. Allow to dry.

What you need:
- Tracing paper
- Scissors
- 1x2-inch rectangular art gum eraser (available at office and art stores)
- Pencil
- Sharp knife
- One 5x12-inch piece of blue cardstock
- Light blue rubber stamp ink pad
- Fine light blue glitter
- Metal dimensional alphabet square stickers (available at scrapbooking stores)

tree stamp
shape

JOYOUS NOEL CARD
Greet everyone on your Christmas card list with this clever winter scene sending a holiday message.

 What you do:

Trace the tree pattern, *left,* onto tracing paper. Cut out and draw around the tree onto the front of the eraser. The edges of the tree should just touch the eraser edges. Cut out around the edges with a sharp knife, leaving a raised portion that is in the shape of the tree. Make a few cuts into the tree for texture. Score the cardstock and fold in half. Press the stamp into the ink pad and make tree shapes across the bottom of the card. Using your finger, make a few small fingerprints across the card front. Dust with glitter while still wet. Let dry. Position the letters to spell NOEL on the top of the card.

COUNTRY SANTA CARD

Bring warmth and smiles to all of your friends and family with this delightful Santa greeting card.

 **What you do:**

Color copy or scan the Country Santa art on *page 153* onto cardstock. Cut out. Set aside. Score and fold the red cardstock to make a 7x6-inch card. Center and glue the art on the front of the card using the glue stick. Use the crafts glue to run a bead of glue all around the edge of the image. Dust the line of glue with fine blue glitter. Allow to dry.

 What you need:
- **Country Santa Art on page 153**
- **7x12-inch piece of red cardstock**
- **Scissors**
- **Glue stick**
- **Crafts glue**
- **Fine blue glitter**

To Give

This card is so beautiful and unique it makes a lovely framed piece. Place the card in a simple frame and wrap it in holiday tissue and a big white bow for a wonderful surprise.

What you need:

- One 11x8½ piece of medium-tone purple cardstock
- One 4x6-inch piece of dark purple cardstock
- Decorative-edge scissors
- Glue stick
- Silver vellum stickers with images and sayings such as Paintworks Merry Christmas Silver #700-144
- Crafts glue
- Fine light purple glitter

PRETTY AND PURPLE GREETING

Two colors of cardstock and silver stickers make this card one to make by the dozens.

What you do:

Score and fold the medium-tone purple cardstock in half. Place the fold at the top. Using the decorative-edge scissors, trim the darker purple cardstock to measure 3¼x5¼ inches. Center and glue the dark cardstock on top of the light cardstock. Place the stickers around the edge and a large "Merry Christmas" in the center. Add a bow or other sticker in the left top corner. Place a little crafts glue on your finger and make polka dots on the card front. Put a little glue on the bow. Dust the card front with glitter. Allow to dry.

CHRISTMAS ALL AROUND

This beautiful holiday medallion card will be kept and displayed for Christmases to come.

❄ What you do:

Color copy the desired Medallion Art on *page 154* onto cardstock. Cut out with decorative-edge scissors. Set aside with wrong side up. Cut a $4^7/_8$-inch circle from the teal cardstock. Lay this circle to the right side of the medallion circle. Connect the two circles by laying the small teal rectangle between the circles, overlapping each circle by $^1/_2$ inch. Glue the tab to each circle. Fold the tab in half bringing the medallion art to the front of the card. Write desired message with gold fine line pen on inside of card.

❄ What you need:
- **Art from page 154**
- **Decorative-edged scissors**
- **One 5-inch piece of teal cardstock**
- **One 1x2-inch rectangle of teal cardstock**
- **Glue stick**
- **Gold fine line pen**

GOLDEN SNOWFLAKE GREETING

A snowflake stamp and some golden ink make this card spell a Merry Christmas!

What you do:

Cut the black cardstock in half. Score and fold to make a 6x6-inch card. Glue the gold stripe paper on top of the black paper about 1¹⁄₂ inches from the top. Glue the red cardstock in the middle of the gold paper. Using the Merry Christmas stamp and gold ink pad, stamp Merry Christmas on the red cardstock. Using the snowflake stamp and gold ink pad, stamp the snowflakes on top of all the papers, overlapping the stamp over the edges of the papers. Dust the snowflakes with glitter while still wet. Allow to dry.

So Easy

Make these clever cards for everyone on your Christmas list. Cut all of the cardstock pieces at one time and glue together. Then, in assembly line fashion, stamp and glitter all of them at once. You'll have plenty of cards for your favorite people in no time!

146

CHRISTMAS PAST

Cherish the Christmases of long ago by color-copying some of the heirlooms you treasure.

❋ What you need:
- **White and green cardstock**
- **Red patterned cardstock**
- **Gray chalk**
- **Color copies of vintage fabrics**
- **Computer; fonts**
- **Glue stick**
- **Black photo corners**
- **Scissors; adhesive**

❋ What you do:

Select black and white photos to contrast with the colors of the vintage pieces that you choose. For more ideas, see details, *below.*

Chalk the white edges of the layout for an aged look.

Color copy a vintage apron, cut it out, and use to hold a favorite family recipe.

Every Christmas was a wonderful time with my Grandparents. Everyone in the family was a good cook, and Grandma's famous ice box cookies were a favorite. I always remember both Mother and Grandma wearing a pretty Christmas apron during the holidays and setting the table on a bright printed tablecloth.

Color copy a vintage tablecloth and cut out shapes to use as the main motif on the pages.

Grandpa and Grandma Schipull
In their home at Christmastime.

Choose a subtly patterned paper to coordinate with your vintage motif. In this case, the diamond motif provided a coordinating color and was easy to trim to create a border.

MADRIGAL FEAST
A very special occasion deserves royal treatment.

❄ What you need:
- **Cardstock in shades of blue**
- **Preprinted gold letters**
- **3-D stickers**
- **Wide gold ribbon**
- **Small brads**
- **Gold embossed paper**
- **Adhesive spacers**
- **Scissors; pencil; glue adhesive; decorative ruler**

❄ What you do:

Create a background of stage curtains by cutting a 12x12-inch sheet of cardstock in half. Trim the bottom of each half using a decorative ruler. For more ideas, see details, *below.*

Add a strip of wide decorative ribbon to the outside edges.

Use a pre-printed title in gold to match gold embellishments.

To create title "banner", scan and shrink the actual program used at the event.

For medallions, cut squares from gold print paper, mat on cardstock, then mat again on gold squares. Mount with adhesive spacers.

Create a journaling box that looks like a scroll. Mount over a strip of cardstock secured with brads.

SANTA CAME TO SEE US!

Scrapbook a page about Santa's visit using lots of bright motifs in red and green.

❄ What you need:
- **Red, green, and brown cardstock**
- **Patterned cardstock**
- **Flower punch**
- **Gold brads**
- **Adhesive spacers**
- **Computer; fonts**
- **Scissors**
- **Adhesive**

❄ What you do:

Use many photos from that special party by grouping them in grid-like style. Make your own holiday motifs or choose precut ones that suit the layouts. For more ideas, see details, *below.*

To create packages, cut squares and rectangles from red and green patterned cardstock. Cut narrow strips for ribbons; use a flower punch for the bows.

Repeat the "brick" theme by using a grid style for six similar pictures. Trim the photos to the same size.

Add details such as logs and stockings. Adhere with adhesive spacers. Use brads as stocking holders. Add a chimney to the top of the fireplace.

Draw a simple fireplace (or enlarge a die-cut to get the basic shape) and cut out from brown cardstock. Cut little rectangle "bricks" and glue on the fireplace.

149

CAROLS FOR CHRISTMAS

Choose colors that compliment the patina of vintage music—black and ecru—and add a touch of gold to make this rich-looking scrapbook page.

❄ What you need:
- **Black cardstock**
- **Vintage sheet music**
- **Wide and fine gold ribbon**
- **Adhesive spacers**
- **Black chalk**
- **Brad**
- **Gold pen**
- **Scissors; adhesive**

❄ What you do:

Use vintage sheet music as the theme for a special holiday concert scrapbooking page. For more ideas, see details, *below.*

The title of one of the books doubles as the title of the layout.

Chalk the edges of the papers for a worn look.

Add a strip of gold ribbon to the top of the layout. Use elements from the copied music to embellish the corner. Add a gold ribbon bow.

Color copy vintage sheet music to be the basic element on the page.

Make a small journaling block and embellish with holly leaves. Fold one corner inward and secure with a gold brad. Chalk in black.

CHRISTMAS SNOW

Make a winter wonderland with your talent and our exclusive Snow Fun Art on pages 156-157.

 What you do:

Use the art provided on pages 156-157 to create these winter layouts. For more ideas, see details, *below.*

What you need:
- **Cardstock in shades of blue**
- **Printed vellum**
- **Snow Fun Art on pages 156-157**
- **Blue eyelets**
- **Blue ribbon**
- **Snowflake punches**
- **Hanging tags**
- **Scissors; adhesive**
- **Computer; fonts**

Create a large frame for your focal point photo using the art provided.

Arrange photos over a square of dotted vellum (chosen to pick up the snow motif). Adhere vellum by hiding adhesive behind photos.

Add ribbon to the tag, and secure to your layout with adhesive spacers.

Finish the layout by adding punched snowflakes.

Cut up a strip of the art provided and arrange it casually across the bottom strip. Add an eyelet to the edge.

In the winter of 1986, Michael and Elizabeth went skiing for the first time. It was Christmas and the morning snow was beautiful. Our friend Judy was there to visit and we all went to Humboldt to try to ski. Roger and Michael were the brave ones. Lizzy, Judy, and I had hot chocolate!

- **Dark green, black, and rust red cardstock**
- **Die cut letters**
- **Folk Art provided on page 155**
- **Paper punches**
- **Scissors**
- **Adhesive**

LIKE FAMILY

Give a warm folk art look to your scrapbook page using the exclusive Folk Art Trims on page 155.

❋ What you do:

Visually separate the layout into two vertical halves. Place pieces of art on one side and a single photo framed in the matching border on the other. For more ideas, see details, *below*.

Use die-cut letters to create a title for the layout. Place a punched quilt block under the first and last letters for an added touch.

Create a quilt effect for the left side of your layout positioning the art pieces in a quilt-like placement.

Add some punched pieces to the artwork such as punched holly leaves, little Christmas trees, and punched dots.

Cut a journaling block for the bottom left of the layout. Add photo corners.

Sarah is the sweetest of girls. She loves her kittens and her music! We love Sarah (and her mom and dad) just like family.

Country Santa Art

Color copy at 100% for Santa Place Card on
page 101, and for Country Santa Greeting Card on *page 143*.

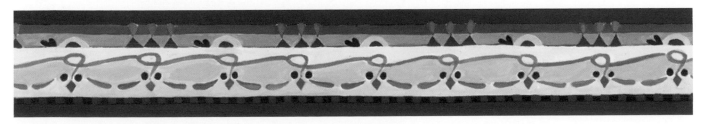

Holiday Border Art

Color copy at 100% for Napkin Ring on *page 101*.

Medallion Art A

Color copy at 75% for Patterned Coasters on *page 98* and at 100% for Greeting Card on *page 145*

Medallion Art B

Color copy at 75% for coasters on *page 98* and at 100% for card on *page 145*

Folk Art Trims

Color copy at 100%
for scrapbook page on
page 152

Snow Fun Art

Color copy at 100% for
Mitten Wrap on *page 84* and
Christmas Snow on *page 151*.

Index

SOURCES

Edible Glitter, Dragees, Luster Dust, Cookie Cutters, Colored Sugars
Maid of Scandinavia by Sweet Celebrations (800) 328-6722
www.sweetc.com

Knitted Hat and Mittens
Classic Elite Yarns
(800) 343-0308
E-mail: classicelite@aol.com

Micro Beads
Art Accents
www.artaccents.net

Ribbon
C.M. Offray & Sons
(800) 344-5533

Spray Paint
Design Master Paints
www.backgroundstobasics.com

Stickers
Printworks
Santa Fe Spring, CA

EK Success Ltd.
P.O. Box 1141, Clifton, NJ
07014-1141
www.eksuccess.com

If you like this book, look for these other books by Carol Field Dahlstrom and Brave Ink Press:
**Simply Christmas
Christmas-Make it Sparkle
An Ornament a Day**

To order books or to send your comments or suggestions, e-mail us at braveink@aol.com

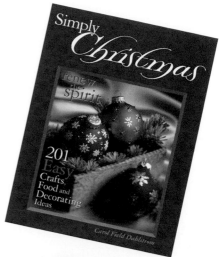

ACKNOWLEDGEMENTS

Lyne Neymeyer is a talented graphic artist as well as a photographer and university professor. Her sense of design and use of color have set her apart as an outstanding book designer for more than 20 years.

Pete Krumhardt is known globally for his amazing photographic talent. His use of light and his vast understanding of nature are evident in the thousands of photos that appear in major magazines and books.

Susan Cornelison is a professional book illustrator and is best known for her charming mixed-media illustrations in children's books. Her work appears in greeting cards as well as many quality book products.

Jennifer Petersen has an unusual talent for making her decorated food become beautiful art. Her work can be seen in cooking magazines and books throughout the country.

A special thank you to BJ Berti for her continued support and creative ideas in the making of this book.

This book is dedicated to my husband, Roger, and our children,
Michael and Elizabeth, who make every day Christmas for me.

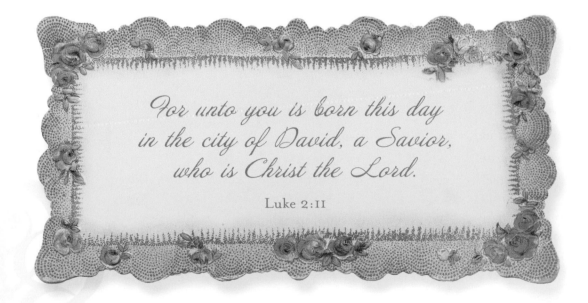

For unto you is born this day
in the city of David, a Savior,
who is Christ the Lord.

Luke 2:11